DIGCITKIDS

LESSONS LEARNING SIDE-BY-SIDE, TO EMPOWER OTHERS AROUND THE WORLD

MARIALICE CURRAN, PH.D.

CURRAN DEE

educational matchmaker

DigCitKids
Marialice B.F.X. Curran, Ph.D. and Curran Dee

Published by EduMatch®
PO Box 150324, Alexandria, VA 22315 www.edumatch.org

These books are available at special discounts when purchased in quantities of 10 or more for use as premiums, promotions fundraising, and educational use. For inquiries and details, contact the publisher: sarah@edumatch.org.

DEDICATION

In many ways, growing up in the digital age is like exploring the new frontier for the first time. As a mother and son team when we began our journey, we didn't find an official guidebook or map to steer us, but plenty of people helped us navigate the way. Just as first-time parents bringing a baby home from the hospital might wish for a manual after the delivery, it's really family and friends who provide the support. To all the parents out there, especially my own, thank you for being the first teachers in our lives; our love for learning begins at home with you.

Since my college campus was like a second home, Curran and I would also like to thank all the undergraduate and graduate students that I have had in my classes spanning a decade, who are truly at the roots of our story. We'd also like to thank everyone who ever took the time to write a blog comment, join us on Skype calls, engage with us on social media, and inspire us to learn together. Your time and contributions made our connected learning journey more meaningful, and although countless people have supported us along the way, we'd specifically like to recognize and thank Hayley Brown, Jaime Donally, Derek Larson, and Sarah Thomas for being more than just our Personal Learning Network (PLN), but for becoming part of our online family.

Lastly, none of this would be possible without the unwavering support from a husband and father, so thank you Sean/Dad for being our loudest cheerleader. And to all the contributors to this book — we love learning alongside you. Thank you for sharing your stories on how you embed digital citizenship into your everyday routines. As the saying and hashtag go, we are # BetterTogether!

CONTENTS

PREFACE

DigCitKids is digital citizenship for kids by kids. **DigCitKids** solve real problems in local, global, and digital communities.

Although Curran's connected learning journey began when he was just a preschooler, he did not start DigCitKids until his first TEDxYouth talk when he was nine years old. Before that, he actively joined his mother, Marialice, as she prepared for and taught both her undergraduate and graduate teacher education courses in instructional technology. Sometimes he would attend classes and work with the teacher candidates; other times he'd get involved with edtech projects at home like Skype calls and Twitter chats with classrooms around the world. It was a natural progression that began side-by-side, as a mother and son blog, which ultimately developed into DigCitKids. At the TEDxYouth event, Curran noticed that he was the youngest student speaker and questioned why a youth event only had high school students and adults talking about student voice. This was the impetus behind starting DigCitKids as a way to ensure that students, even our youngest learners, had opportunities to inspire and empower other students.

As the Chief Kid Officer (CKO) of DigCitKids, Curran's message highlights, "The next CEO is a kid," and that we are waiting too long to engage kids into making a *DigCitImpact*[1] where they think globally and act locally. This call to action reminds us that digital citizenship isn't just a lesson plan; digital citizenship is something we can and need to embed into everything we do at school, at home, and at work.

Curran is currently a sixth grader who plays hockey, soccer, and basketball; he's a gamer, as well as an international speaker and a student Ignite speaker at ISTE.

He is also a two-time TEDxYouth speaker, and his talk has been used as professional development for educators as a way to encourage connected learning for students everywhere: "If you want us to learn about the world, we need to learn *with* the world."

Unfortunately, Curran is a connected learner in an unconnected classroom; his definition of digital access goes beyond access to technology and has inspired him to advocate for connected learning opportunities in classrooms around the world. Inspired by Africa's Next CEO conference,[2] Curran believes the next CEO is a kid, so we need to provide access for connected learning opportunities for *all* students everywhere.

This book is a compilation of stories, starting with our own mother and son story, and shares examples from both parents and educators on how they embed digital citizenship at home and in the classroom. The stories highlight how learning together and talking *with* kids — not at kids — is something we all can do, every single day.

FOREWORD

Let's start with the meaning of the title of this book, which also explains how all the authors were gathered for this compilation. DigCitKids is about our youngest generation understanding and being guides in the explorations of the online world and learning side-by-side with parents, educators, and other kids how to be responsible digital citizens online.

More than a decade ago, Marialice embarked on her journey as a promoter of the concept of digital citizenship. As her son Curran began to explore the online world side-by-side with his mom, he too became an advocate and leader in the digital citizenship movement, eventually traveling with his mom worldwide to sponsor digital citizenship events, and taking on at a young age keynoting at local and international conferences, in addition to becoming one of the youngest TEDxYouth speakers.

Through their journey together, the mother-and-son team met with and collaborated with a host of people, also leaders in the digital citizenship movement. As Curran noted early on, kids also need to be at the forefront of this movement, and the contributors to this collaborative work commonly espouse giving ownership of the movement to the young generation.

In this book, you will read powerful stories told by digital citizenship believers worldwide, stretching as far as India, Australia, Nigeria, Spain, Scotland, Mexico, as well as within the United States. That this movement has spread worldwide is attributed largely to the unwavering support of Marialice and Curran to see their dream of working side-by-side globally, locally, and digitally result in a new generation of responsible, caring digital citizens.

By learning side-by-side as you go through this book, you will witness powerful personal stories of global connectedness and digital responsibility, as well as take away practical ideas you can implement with your own children, children in schools, and children in our communities. You will learn ways to make today's children global leaders and will partner with people to guide your journey. The authors offer links to a wealth of resources and varied ways to stay in touch with them. So begin your journey now, exploring paths to enhance your skills as a digital citizenship advocate and tour guide. Welcome aboard to your personalized and connected learning venture, and stay in touch with the authors both while reading the book and beyond.

Judy Arzt, Ph.D.
Instructional Technology Professor

CHAPTER ONE
DIGCITKIDS: OUR STORY

Dr. Marialice B.F.X. Curran and Curran Dee, United States

Digital Citizenship Institute[1] and DigCitKids[2]

Marialice and her son, Curran are internationally recognized as a mother/son team. As digital citizenship pioneers, they promote connected learning through global collaboration as a way to educate and empower local, global, and digital communities. Professionally, Marialice has served as an associate professor, middle school teacher, and principal, and is a champion of student voice.

PARENTING AND TEACHING IN THE DIGITAL AGE

Marialice

Parenting in the digital age is not as much about the technology as it is about parenting. It's not just about monitoring, it's about mentoring. You don't need to be a technology expert, you need to be a parent — and just as my parents taught me life skills like how to tie my shoes, ride a bike, and learn to cross the street, I learned all these things by doing them *with* my parents by my side, modeling, and teaching me. These same rules apply to parenting in the digital age. I literally and figuratively held (and continue to hold) the back of Curran's bike seat as he learns how to balance and become independent both on and offline.

As Claudio Zavala (the author of Chapter 8) and I once discussed on Voxer, a walkie-talkie app,[3] I like to think of parenting in the digital age as learning how to ride a bike. Our first experience on a bike might be on a seat that, these days, can either be on the handlebars, behind the parent's seat, or in a pop-up tent that rides behind the parent's bike. Riders then graduate and learn to balance on bikes without pedals, which leads to pedal bikes and sometimes our biking experience might also include tricycles, big wheels, bikes with training wheels, and tandem/buddy bikes. There are so many biking options like unicycles, adapted bicycles for mobility and special needs, bikes that you can pedal with your arms, dirt bikes, touring bikes, off-road bikes, mountain bikes, hybrids, or cruisers that make learning to ride a bike accessible for all.

Recently, I shared this analogy during a keynote highlighting the underlying message about the power of continuously learning together, side-by-side. Just like learning how to ride a bike, we all learn in our own way, at our own pace on a bike that meets our needs. I can close my eyes and see my neighborhood where I learned how to ride my bike. I can feel and anticipate the pitch of the driveway, the curves in the sidewalk, and even the uneven surfaces that I tried to avoid. I was a late bloomer and remember "walking my bike" to the neighbors' so I could park it with the pile of other bikes. I also remember my parents, neighbors, and friends holding the back of my seat, running next to me, encouraging me and giving me advice on how to balance the bike on my own—and I can hear them all cheering the day that I finally was riding solo!

The expression *it takes a village* is just as relevant today as it was when I was growing up. Just like the "neighborhood watch" when I was a kid, we still need our neighborhood to guide us both on and offline, to model how to navigate and balance the challenges we all face in life. Just like riding a bike, we all need to learn the rules of the road with a community by our side, so that one day when we find ourselves on a new road or path, we'll be better prepared for whatever lies ahead.

This is exactly how our mother and son digital citizenship journey began. In many ways, our story is what personalized learning looks like in action at home. We share our story not as a one-size-fits-all type of model, but as an inspiration for you to do and learn things in your own way, with your community by your side at home, at school, and at work.

> *Just like learning how to ride a bike, our children need us to run next to them as they figure out how to balance and be independent. As part of digital parenting, it is critical for our children to have someone holding the back of the bike seat as they set out on their online journey.*

THE BEGINNING OF OUR MOTHER AND SON DIGITAL CITIZENSHIP JOURNEY

Marialice

It all began very naturally. At home, we went on nature walks, conducted science experiments, and learned everything we could about dinosaurs and animals. I took the lead from my son, and our adventures were about instilling wonder, curiosity, and awe about the world around us. We'd pack our explorer's backpack with a compass, bug boxes, magnifying lens, nets, coloring pencils, a journal, binoculars, and animal identification tracking books (in case we needed to identify a paw print). Our adventures were about learning together, and one question led us to other questions. Since our extended families lived in other parts of the country, in the summer of 2012, we decided to start a blog[4] so our families could learn with us. *Adventures with the Explorer's Backpack* is the first time we began to document our mother and son story together side-by-side, but our adventures began long before we started to blog.

As a mom of a toddler, I was also the faculty member on record in the School of Education for the Educational Technology program at the University of Saint Joseph in West Hartford, Connecticut. In my role as a professor, I began to blog professionally by 2011, and it wasn't long before I was blogging about the Utter Joy of Curiosity[5] and the adventures with my son as a way to help my elementary preservice teachers understand the importance of teaching social studies and science. As I balanced the demands of working and motherhood, there were times out of necessity that I had to bring my son with me to class when he was a baby, toddler, and young child. Sometimes he'd be nuzzled into my neck, not interested in engaging with my students or colleagues, and other times, he engaged actively in the group work happening in class. Over the years, he became a regular on campus, and in many ways, my university became like a second home to him as he joined both undergraduate and graduate students in ongoing projects.

In the beginning, in most public situations, he hid behind me, barely made eye contact, and was painfully shy and mute; but in my classroom, he was an active observer who would eagerly participate in the classroom activities. My classes were untraditional, and teacher candidates were live tweeting or on a Skype call or Google Hangout with our iMentors,[6] experts who were virtual mentors to provide connected learning opportunities as part of field observations and practicums. It was generally busy and loud, but he'd inevitably join a small group and would learn alongside my undergraduate and graduate students on the assignment for the day. Although he didn't usually speak in these classes, he was always thoroughly engaged.

This was also evident at home where he was interested in helping me prepare to teach my courses. He wanted to know about the projects happening and sat right next to me, learning side-by-side. My under-graduate and graduate students were blog buddies with many class-room blogs, and each week we'd leave comments for the student bloggers. At home, he visited the classroom blogs and helped me compose comments. Looking back at our journey together, there's no surprise that he became actively involved with my work.

Curran

Before I was in school, we always did things together whether it was going on adventures, blogging, trying out new edtech tools, Twitter chats, Skype calls, or online conferences. Learning was something we did together, and a lot of the learning began outside, like when we were in San Diego and we were comparing and contrasting the East Coast and West Coast or when I went lobstering with my friend chil-dren's author, Jerry Pallotta.[7] What started offline was shared online, and everything was a teachable moment.

I attended undergraduate and graduate courses where I worked on projects with my mom's students. Some projects were online, and we used tech tools, and other projects were science experiments or social studies adventures like Geocaching.[8] We Skyped with classrooms, and that was always fun because we met a lot of people and learned a lot of things. Some of those online connections eventually became what we called, my online neighborhood watch too. With my mom, I picked trusted adults in my online life that I could turn to if I ever needed help, just like we did with neighbors who live near us.

Marialice

In November 2013, I wanted to create a teachable moment for my undergraduate students on the permanency of their decisions made online, as well as the consequences of an unintended audience. What I soon realized was that my role as an educator and as a parent would coincide.

I thought if Jules Verne[9] could travel around the world in 80 days, how long would it take a tweet to do the same. I wondered how quickly a single tweet could be retweeted around the world, and where would it travel. The resulting project was a Tweet Seen Around the World,[10] a combination of Jules Verne's travels and the famous statement marking the beginning of the American Revolution, "The shot heard around the world." That one tweet traveled to all 50 states and was read in 30 countries and six out of the seven continents in 24 hours. As the 264 responses were rapidly pinging on my computer, Curran, only a 1st grader at the time, was mesmerized. After each ping, he'd want to know the location. "We made it to Indonesia," and he'd echo with such excitement in his voice, "We made it to Indonesia! Where's Indonesia?" This experience with my son surprisingly became an invaluable lesson in geography, as well as a teachable moment for my students to understand the power of social media as a learning tool.

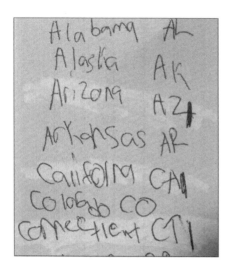

Curran

My connected learning journey really began when my mom sent one tweet around the world when I was in the first grade. Although the tweet heard around the world project was a lesson for students enrolled in my mom's college course, it was my first official digital citizenship lesson.

That one tweet traveled around the world in **24 hours** and received **2,274 views and 264 comments**. This is the power of **publishing** our work to an authentic audience.

We took out a world map so I could find, record, and tally every location.

The tweet traveled to all 50 states, Canada, Mexico, Costa Rica, Australia, Singapore, England, Ireland, Wales, Scotland, Sweden, Belgium, Holland, South Africa, Finland, Denmark, Italy, France, Dubai, Russia, Indonesia, Germany, New Zealand, Vietnam, Korea, China, Japan, and Romania.

That one tweet was the best geography lesson.

The next day, I wanted to keep learning about the world, and I asked my mom if I could start my own blog, Around the World With Curran.[11]

While I was learning in a traditional classroom, I was blogging at home.

By the age of seven, I knew what student choice and student voice looked like at home, and I understood the power of social media to connect with a global audience to make my learning authentic. At home, alongside my mom, I learned how to write quality blog comments from Linda Yollis's students in California[12]; I learned about classroom blogs, Kidblog and the #Comments4Kids blog from William Chamberlain[13] and Kathy Cassidy,[14] and her students in Canada inspired me to share my voice with the world.

LEARNING DIFFERENTLY IN DELIBERATE AND MEANINGFUL WAYS

Curran

At the end of the first grade, our class was assigned a project on rainforest animals. We were given a packet full of instructions including questions to answer, but I came home and blogged about my project. I asked my readers to share what rainforest animal they would research and why. Just like my first blog post, my rainforest animal post received a lot of comments.

I looked up every location on the map and researched each rainforest animal that was suggested. I learned about rainforest animals like the Okapi, Hyacinth Macaw, Jambu Fruit Dove, Aye-Aye, Glass Frog, Candiru fish, Bengal tiger, Amazon Vittata, Toucan parrot, the Cloudrunner (commonly known as the cloud rat), Leaf Cutter ants, Hawaiian Happy Face Spider, Pink River Dolphin, Poison Dart Frog, and many other rainforest animals. I put all the rainforest animals into categories until I came up with my top 10, my top 5, and finally my top choice -- the binturong. I would never have known about the binturong if I was not for a comment from Peru about the bearcat that had a prehensile tail and smelled like popcorn.

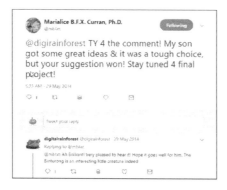

I wish my entire first grade could have had the same experience I did, but they just completed and passed in the packet of worksheets.

Marialice

When Curran came home with the packet of directions for the rainforest project, he said that he didn't want to just learn about the rainforest animals on the teacher's list, but that he wanted to learn about *all* the animals in the rainforest. He asked if he could blog about it and if I would tweet out his blog post — amazing that a first grader could understand the power of social media as a learning tool. He blogged, *Animals in the Rainforest,*[15] and asked the readers to make suggestions on which rainforest animal they would want to research. Just like finding all the locations on the world map, he researched every single animal that was suggested. As a mother, I was so happy that he was so involved and engaged in this project, but as an educator, my heart broke because every student should have the same opportunities to learn this way.

As a college professor, my syllabi and courses were personalized, and I tried to model why publishing your learning was better than passing in the same assignment on the same day. I would begin every new semester by saying, "If you enrolled in this course expecting me to teach you something, I'm sorry to say, but you are in the wrong course." I would follow this up with, "But, if you are willing to trust me, I promise you, I'll learn *with* you, every step of the way." No matter what age you are, building trust is the foundation for learning. In a blog post[16] about the first time Curran jumped off a diving board, I'm reminded of the connection to learning how to ride a bike. What's the common denominator? Knowing someone you trust is by your side:

 We ask our students to take risks in our classrooms all the time, but what do we do to create a safe environment? How do we help our students feel safe enough in our classrooms to jump off the diving board?

Imagine if learning looked like Curran's rainforest animal project. We'd have engaged and empowered learners at home, at school, and at work.

I never anticipated that we would ever tell our story together publicly, but in October 2015, as I was walked up onto the stage to give the closing remarks at the inaugural DigCitSummit,[17] to my surprise, Curran followed me on stage. I turned and asked if he had something he wanted to share, and he nodded and told me he wanted to share his binturong blog story with the audience. I fed him the sentence starters, and he told his story, and at the end, he leaned into the microphone and said, "thank you."

That day, I learned such a valuable lesson. Every one of our students has a story to tell; they just need an invitation to tell it. When we think of our quietest learners, how do we support them, make them feel safe, and provide opportunities to bring out the very best in them? The answer is simple: our students deserve opportunities at school to connect and collaborate with other students and classrooms around the world.

Curran

This was my first time on stage. I knew a lot of people at the DigCit-Summit because many were my mom's students and others were part of my Personal Learning Network (PLN) and online neighborhood watch. The session before the closing remarks, I saw Timmy Sullivan,[18] a high school junior, present with his teacher, and I knew I wanted to tell my story.

When my mom walked on the stage, I followed her, and that was the moment we officially became a co-presenting team.

From Marialice: Every student has a story to tell; they just need an invitation to tell it. Send your invitation today by creating a parent/child social media account together or a classroom account for your students. Make real-world connections at home, at school and, at work.

From Curran: Even the quietest students have something to say, and even though we might not raise our hand to participate in class, there are other ways to engage us in the learning process.

THE IMPORTANCE OF CONNECTED LEARNING

Marialice

The ripple effect an idea can have on the world has always astounded me. I've compared the effect to skipping stones in the water; the stones skip and create ripples in motion. As an educator, this ripple effect happened to me during the fall of 2009 when I was invited into Tracy Mercier's (@vr2ltch) third-grade classroom to participate in a student tech event. As I sat on a rug with several third-graders who were busy typing on their netbooks, they asked me to spell my name. They quickly informed me they were checking if I was making socially responsible decisions online. I gulped. This was the first time I was conscious of anyone doing a Google search on me. *What would they find?* Luckily, I grew up in the '80s, and my adolescence was not permanently captured online. The third graders could only find evidence of my work as a university faculty member, but this made me very aware that I had a responsibility to help prepare future teachers to meet the needs of today's students. I spent that year creating and developing the first three-credit digital citizenship course *specifically focused on digital citizenship* in the country.

By the fall of 2010, I was teaching the new digital citizenship course, and around the same time, a tragic incident involving social media, homophobia, and invasion of privacy happened. Tyler Clementi,[19] a college freshman at Rutgers, took his own life after he discovered that his roommate had secretly recorded and posted videos. There have been many suicides that have affected me, but for the first time, as a relatively new mother, it became personal. I blogged about it, Dinosaurs and Tiaras: Facing Intolerance:[20]

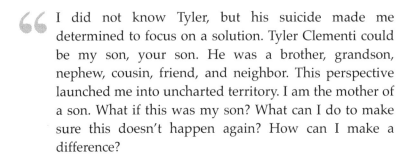

> I did not know Tyler, but his suicide made me determined to focus on a solution. Tyler Clementi could be my son, your son. He was a brother, grandson, nephew, cousin, friend, and neighbor. This perspective launched me into uncharted territory. I am the mother of a son. What if this was my son? What can I do to make sure this doesn't happen again? How can I make a difference?

I was determined to do more and began creating a new course for my university's First Year Seminar Program for incoming college freshmen, Pleased to Tweet You: Are You a Socially Responsible Digital Citizen? I knew this course would be an opportunity for the college freshmen to create a foundation for their undergraduate experience, but I also thought connecting beyond our campus walls would provide an invaluable connected learning opportunity. Prior to the course beginning, I blogged[21] that summer and asked if any other classroom would like to join us. There were many responses, but Beth Sanders from Birmingham, Alabama made it work for her high school juniors. For an entire semester, geography was not an issue as our two classes collaborated over Twitter and Skype to define what it meant to be a digital citizen in the 21st century. The final product was the iCitizen Project[22] where the students shared the importance of thinking and *acting* at local, global, and digital levels simultaneously.

Although I originally hoped that the course would create a student solution towards cyberbullying, what both classes demonstrated was the beginning of moving from a reactive to a proactive approach as everyone involved with the iCitizen Project experienced the difference between being an active citizen not just a resident, an enabler of change, not just a bystander. They focused on empathy and learned the importance of humanizing the person next to them, around the world, as well as across the screen.

As the semester unfolded, the students in both classrooms took active roles leading Twitter chats for teachers, creating public service announcements, and ultimately being the voice behind our first live-streamed event, the iCitizenship Town Hall Meeting,[23] which was the first chapter for ultimately hosting the inaugural Digital Citizenship Summit in October 2015.

Curran

Since the first grade, I have used a variety of tools to connect and learn with the world. I've presented at EdChange Global, Global Maker Day, EduMatch, and Pass the Scope EDU. I've moderated dozens of Twitter chats and provided professional development for teachers. I've shared my story at TEDxYouth, DigCitSummits around the world in the UK, Nigeria, Mexico, Spain, and Ireland, and presented at Twitter Head-quarters and ISTE, as well as other conferences—but all these amazing connected learning opportunities have happened outside of school.

I'm a connected student in an unconnected classroom.

Why does school ask us to learn in isolation?

The quote, "No man is an island" needs to apply to students, too. I don't want to be on an island at school—I want to be connected with classrooms and students around the world. I know what connected classrooms look like because I join them from home.

Marialice

What are the benefits of global education? It unites us. Geography is no longer an obstacle, and with Google translator, language is no longer a barrier for us to connect either. When we were in Nigeria for DigCitSummitNG, we met two brothers, and Curran invited them to join us for the Global Read Aloud.[24] As we all know, one book can change a life, but an opportunity to breakdown classroom walls and learn and connect with other students and classrooms connects you with the world from the palm of your hand.

Curran

There are so many ways you can learn about the world *with* the world both at home and at school. The Global Read Aloud is just one way to experience the power of connected learning. When we connected with the kids in Nigeria, I learned that more things make us alike than make us different. No matter where you live or what language you speak, kids are kids.

One of our favorite connected learning stories happened during the Skypeathon a few years ago. On St. Andrew's Day, Mrs. Jalland's class in Scotland sang the "Flower of Scotland.[25]" How would we ever have known about this Scottish holiday if we didn't join the Skypeathon?

This is what learning should look like in every classroom every single day.

Marialice and Curran

As we reflect on our connected learning journey together, it started early, and it began offline. We encourage you to begin this conversation at home by doing simple things like going to the ballgame device-free [26] so you can experience some JOMO (Joy of Missing Out) as you allow yourself to be completely in the moment and present. Decide as a family to keep *all* devices (not just the kid's devices) downstairs at night and return to saying good morning and good night to a family member instead of your device. Go device free during dinners and family visits because being unplugged is vital. Remember, our kids are watching us, and we need to be the best role models that we can be, so call a family meeting and decide what works best for you and your family and just be willing to learn together.

> *From Marialice: This isn't about the technology, this is a change in mindset. We need to be willing to learn alongside our students in the classroom and our children and teens at home.*

> *From Curran: Don't ask us to memorize things we can Google because we need to learn about the world with the world. We need to publish our work, not fill in worksheets that we pass in to our teachers.*

DIGCITKIDS: DIGITAL CITIZENSHIP FOR KIDS BY KIDS

Curran

By the third grade, I gave my first TEDxYouth talk and shared my story, My Wish: Digital Access For All Students Everywhere.[27] At the time, I noticed that all the student speakers were in high school and the other speakers were all adults, and it made me wonder, "Why does everyone wait to talk to students until they are older," because elementary students just like me have a lot to say. I had noticed that adults were always talking about student voice, but why weren't kids talking about it? Instead of adults empowering kids, I wanted to have kids inspire and empower other kids.

Sharing my story inspired me to want to start my own company, DigCitKids. DigCitKids is digital citizenship for kids by kids.

DigCitKids was created as a way to share our voice with the world, solving problems and creating solutions, and empowering other kids because our online actions can travel around the world to help other kids.

DigCitKids can be done in school and at home.

To #bethatKINDofkid, you can take this pledge inspired by President Barack Obama, "I want us to ask ourselves every day, how are we using technology to make a real difference in people's lives?"[28] DigCitKids asks, "How are **YOU** using technology every day to make a real difference for your community, other kids and the world?"

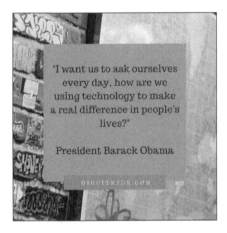

Marialice and Curran

DigCitKids is not a separate lesson plan—not another add-on to the curriculum. Just like digital citizenship is something we all need to model and embed in all grades and contents, it is not a list of materials or procedures. The following chapters will demonstrate how easily digital citizenship happens at home and in school. We hope that you are inspired by our story and the stories in this book. Each author has included practical tips in each chapter to help you begin your own connected learning journey.

We look forward to you sharing your stories with us at digcitkids.com, and be sure to add #DigCitKids and #bethatKINDofkid to your social media posts!

WHAT DOES IT MEAN TO BE DIGCITKIDS APPROVED?

The following chapters are examples of some of our favorite *DigCitKids Approved* stories. To be *DigCitKids Approved* you need to **share** your voice with the world, **solve** problems and create solutions, and **empower** other kids at home and at school.

We use #DigCitKidsApproved when we share stories about kids doing amazing things at home and in classrooms around the world. This blog post highlights 30 students and classrooms that are #DigCitKidsApproved stories. Make sure you connect and learn with these amazing kids![29] We are often asked how can we start? An easy way to begin your own DigCitKids Approved journey is to get kids connecting with senior citizens as a way to learn as a community.

· · ·

Curran

You can start by interviewing your grandparents or any senior citizens in your community. I blogged about my experience, Learning Together: DigCitKids & Cyber Seniors,[30] and here's what I learned:

 Learning is a two-way street. We have a lot to learn from our seniors and they have a lot to learn from us.

We don't even have a home phone, but I learned that calling my grandparents was a better way to discuss this project than sending the online survey. I also learned that seniors don't need to carry a device with them wherever they go. Being connected means something different to them. Being connected to my grandmothers means being present with the people you love.

Marialice

Intergenerational learning is a reminder to us all that learning is a life-long endeavor and that we all are learners regardless of our age. When kids have the opportunity to learn alongside parents (and grandparents) at home, we are providing a community approach towards transforming learners who think critically and act creatively as problem solvers and active citizens.

The Speaking Exchange Project[31] is a great example of kids and senior citizens working together; students in Brazil connected with Americans living in retirement homes. The students in Brazil wanted to learn and practice English to become more fluent, but the entire experience about learning a new language became more about human connections, and as Curran just shared, the learning between the students and seniors was reciprocal. The Cyber Senior project, as previously mentioned, is another example of kids and seniors learning together and is also a reminder that whether you are sitting side-by-side or sitting across a screen, kids and seniors can learn a lot from each other.

On Twitter, connect with Marialice at @mbfxc and Curran at @DigCitKids to continue to learn alongside this mother/son team.

HOW TO GET STARTED

Understanding Our DigCitCommunity Mindset

At the DigCitInstitute, we believe students need the four components referenced in the graphic (empathetic, entrepreneurial, innovative, and inclusive) embedded into K-12 curriculum. We will use DigCitKids Approved examples to highlight what these mindsets look like in action. Regardless of what grade you teach or content you teach, these four mindsets can be integrated into your everyday practice and can be done at school and at home.

When we look at the video *The Future of Work: Will Our Children Be Prepared?*[32], we realize that our K-12 students need to practice and experience empathy every single day because an *Empathetic Mindset* allows our students to understand and share the feelings of others and to walk in their shoes. Take Curran for example, in his TEDxYouth talk, which we explored earlier in the chapter; walk in his shoes and understand his perspective of being a connected learner in an unconnected classroom: My Wish: Digital Access For All Students Everywhere. How are we preparing students for their future? What can we do differently for all of our students to build upon a foundation of empathy?

It was during this TEDxYouth event that Curran looked around and asked, "Why aren't kids talking about student voice?" He was puzzled that a youth event had high school students and adults talking about student voice, but that he was the only student representing elementary school students. It was at this moment when he developed an *Entrepreneurial Mindset* and identified a need and solved it by starting DigCitKids because as he said, "The CEO is a kid and we need more CKOs (Chief Kid Officers) in the world identifying and solving real problems." Embedding an *Entrepreneurial Mindset* into K-12 curriculum provides opportunities for our students to be critical thinkers, and creative problem solvers, who ultimately transform minds, hearts, and attitudes by solving real problems in local, global, and digital communities.

The next layer is focused on an inclusion where access for all, diversity, and equality are at heart. Applying the Universal Design for Learning (UDL) framework, an *Inclusive Mindset* gives all individuals equal opportunities to learn. It promotes personalized learning where all learners and all abilities are recognized, included and valued. UDL provides flexible approaches that can be customized and adjusted for individual needs for everyone to have access to the same learning opportunities. To model this mindset, Curran unexpectedly starts his talk at DigCitSummit in Madrid thanking the sign language interpreters,[33] reminding the audience that this is what access looks like in action because his Dad who is deaf watching the live stream back in the United States can participate fully because of the sign language interpreters. This is a reminder to us all that we need to be mindful that all types of learners have full access to the learning happening in our classrooms.

The last layer needed is an *Innovative Mindset*. Innovators are asking questions that haven't been asked yet — they are the makers, the dreamers, the doers, the futurists who constantly think outside the box and in this case, we'd add outside of the shoebox. When Curran was in the fifth grade, he was assigned a traditional diorama assignment which he adapted into a virtual diorama in Minecraft.[34] Leading with an *Innovative Mindset* allows you to be filled with an insatiable sense of curiosity, and as we all know, one question always leads to another.

The stories included in this book provide concrete examples of DigCit-Kids modeling what the *DigCitCommunity Mindset* looks like when we embed empathy, entrepreneurship, inclusion, and innovation into our daily routines and curriculum. The following chapters are meant to inspire you both at home and at school — including elementary to high school — to invite all students to join us on this learning journey where we are talking with students, not at them.

> *A simple way to begin is to identify a real problem in your community and solve it like fourth-grader Lila Mankad did when she completed her science project which evolved into a Change.org petition, Bag-Free Bayous Houston.[35] This is making a DigCitImpact which inspires and empowers other students around the world.*

Connect on Twitter with the DigCitInstitute at @digcitinstitute and DigCitSummit at @digcitsummit to get involved with these global initiatives.

CHAPTER TWO
BEING A CONNECTED
PARENT

María Zabala, Spain

iWomanish[1]

Maria Zabala is a journalist and mother of three. She writes and talks about family & technology, digital culture, and media literacy. As digcit education advocate, she collaborates with schools, companies, and public institutions.

The Internet has changed the world and the way we do almost everything. How could it not change parenting, childhood, family life, too? **We live surrounded by a constant connection, a fast availability of information, experiences, and goods. And so are our children.** The difference between adults and young generations relies on *perspective* —we remember what it was like before—and on *frontiers*—we tend to differentiate online from offline.

On both accounts, *remembering* and *differentiating*, children and teenagers live in a whole new world of their own. They learn, play, express themselves, and communicate with others with a natural incorporation of gadgets and connection. They have a positive disposition towards technology: a fearless, eager, curiosity-based approach that still doesn't mean they know what they're doing. They are born with no training on patience, self-control, obedience, and decision-making. WE are supposed to be their trainers.

When it comes to technology, it is we parents who put it in their hands first, just as with new food, toys, or plans, with the choice of school or camps. Therefore, we should be the ones to guide the beginning of their digital life and the progressive growth of their connected experience.

Being a connected parent means including the online world in the rest of the education. Not by becoming computer science experts or parental control freaks, not by fostering future tech-talent generations, but by **understanding the world we now live in and raising responsible, creative, healthy, and happy people**.

There is a **public battle** of opinions everywhere, focused on screen time, potential addiction, lost generations, distracted minds, overprotective or non-present parents, lack of face-to-face communication, dangers of the web, cyber-bullying and predators, unauthorized downloads, worsened learning, too much freedom or complete lack of it, hate and violence, and pornography online. We read or hear about it all daily, and then we read or hear about the opportunities of connected classrooms, the need for talent for future jobs, the "digital intelligence." In view of it all, **we either react in fear and ban all technology, or we react in dismissal and hope everything will be alright**.

SCREENS, KNIVES - EDUCATION

Outside of this world of screens, data reveal[2] that knives kill far more people in the United States than rifles do every year. Yet we don't ban **knives** from our homes, because they are a part of our life, and so they become a part of the education we give to our children. As with most of the rest of things in life, **access, intention, and purpose are key**. Parents are the door through which children access most things and the window through which they draw their intention and purpose in life.

When it comes to **knives**, we buy adapted, plastic, colorful knives for our toddlers. And there's a time when we start letting them use normal knives, even a time when we trust in their capacity to use the bigger knives. And if eventually, they cut themselves, we use any kind of bandage available to heal the wound, and then insist on attention and being careful. On the course of this knife-use education, we let them know that a bad use of such a normal tool can end up in real harm. We warn them about mean people who will use knives to hurt others. We share family talks about good manners at the table, how cutlery is used (like knives not being really useful for a soup) and there being a different kind of knife when you eat fish. So it's not so much about the *what*, but more about the *when, how*, and *what for*.

We know how to do this, feel certain and comfortable about it, probably heard it all from our parents before. So we have no doubts about it. Knives exist, can be used for good or wrong, and can become a different kind of tool depending on the moment, the person, the need, *ergo* we EDUCATE our children about it.

And with the rest of **daily life**? It's all about intervention first, autonomy later. Monitor then mentor. We organize playdates or visits to a museum and take our children to piano lessons. We cheer for them in competitions, ask them about friends at school. We don't buy just any toy they wish, don't let them wander around alone at any age. And then we have them do things on their own and occasionally take a look at how they're managing. We say NO to some and YES to some. We are masters at warning then letting then advising then trusting.

HOW COME IT'S SO HARD TO NORMALIZE TECHNOLOGY AND DO THE SAME WITH THEIR DIGITAL GROWTH?

We should **reflect** on what kind of interaction we want our family to have with the digital world, on what concerns us—and then manage a way to address those concerns. We need to see why they really use technology so we can map when and how and where and for what or how long they do it. We need to **understand** threats and opportunities and then talk about both at home. We need to **learn** about this digital world we live in. We need to **normalize** technology as part of our reality and then bring it to real life with our kids, through guidance, coherent decisions, and perseverance.

Being a connected parent means setting **rules** so there can be positive **habits**—with food, with bath time, with homework, with screen time. It means setting an **example** so they can see **balance**—with a healthy diet, with practicing sports, with treating people well, with using technology. It means having **conversations**, so there can be real **communication** (with life at school, with making friends, with becoming responsible and self-reliant, with dealing with online stuff).

It's a bit of choosing the **moment and motive** for connection, about choosing the right content for their age and character. It's about **balancing** ON and OFF, using ON to trigger OFF. It's about understanding who our children are in the playground so we can understand who they'll be on social media. It's about having them learn self-control, learn to wait, think twice, respect, share, and do new things, so they become interesting people. It's about being present and balancing monitoring with mentoring. It's about helping them build who they are and how they express themselves. It's about teaching them to make decisions and be agents of their behavior. It's about raising (smart) people who live and will keep living in a world extremely marked by technology.

Family is the first trench in digital education, so our job now also includes fostering good digital habits and responsible digital behavior. It should not only be about panic and problem, but also about opportunity—opportunity to connect with your children, with each other at home, with the world.

SO, HOW DOES ALL THIS THEORY BECOME A REAL, DAILY OPPORTUNITY TO GUIDE YOUNG GENERATIONS?

I have three children: a teen, a tween, and a child. They are quite different in character and hobbies, so this naturally reflects on how they approach their relationship with technology. I can't be one single digital mentor for the three of them, so I've become an *oracle* of conversations around the topic of '"all things digital."

When my oldest asked for a smartphone, we talked about what he wanted it for and about how it could really improve his life, if it could at all. We talked about "everyone has one" not being a reason, about using it differently than the rest, and about passwords and digital safety. We did not talk about dangers, we talked about opportunities. And we have kept the talk alive ever since. There have been chats about social media and portraying perfect lives, about safe downloads and crediting copyright when necessary, about being an agent of one's attention, time, and habits. He was the one to realize he needed a break from Fortnite and he's the one to search for online information about how to learn video editing on Adobe and iMovie, film script writing, and music composing for Garageband.

When my tween girl asks for a certain popular app or for an Instagram account, we talk about what "the right moment" means. And we frequently chat about the variety of perceptions on love and female attractiveness you can find online. We wonder together about why there are not more women in technology, and we search for videos and tutorials around the things she enjoys the most. She is the one who knows Scratch, the one who best creates complex passwords, and the one understands privacy.

When my youngest is unable to stop watching Netflix, we talk about how much time he dedicates every day to all other types of activities, and then compare. When he states he wants to become a YouTuber, we talk about fame and then search for cool channels and talk some more about anecdotes and inspiration. He draws on paper and on tablet, he plays Minecraft on the console, then builds Minecraft cities with Lego blocks and pretends to be a Minecraft character while playing with friends at school.

I have found that allowing a gradual use of digital tools is the right way for my children and me. I have found that being available and open to talk about their use of technology without judging them makes it easier for them to discover the difference between doing what "everybody does" and doing "something only I can do." And all these chats, all these conversations, allow for funny, constructive and — I hope — efficient family knowledge about a safe, positive, creative, and responsible use of technology. This is what I understand as raising digital citizens.

> *Let's not forget the kids we were and, in a way, still are, so that we can be the parents our children need... today.*

Connect with Maria at @iWomanish to continue to learn alongside her.

CHAPTER THREE
THE GREAT INDIAN DIGITAL FAMILY

Jyoti Chopra, India

SDGs For Children[1]

Jyoti Chopra, her son, Ayush, and daughter Ananya team up as a connected family to foster digital citizenship by promoting socially responsible and safe use of the Internet including social media. They epitomise a successful parent-child partnership in making effective use of digital media tools to turn Netizens into responsible, collaborative, global citizens, passionate about the Sustainable Development Goals (SDGs).

Like many young teens, Ayush loves to unwind, play squash, browse the web, text, chat, share, and so on. But unlike his peers, he's an internationally known speaker on the involvement of kids in social causes and promotion of Sustainable Development Goals (SDGs) as set forth by the United Nations (UN).

Ayush works alongside his mother, Jyoti Chopra, who works as Director IT, spearheading digital transformation at a direct selling company in India. "I strongly believe that we should not resist the change that cyber world and social media have already brought about in our daily lives. The need is only to channelize this technological change in the right direction for the greater good," says the mother with a perpetual, endearing smile. Jyoti adds that we have no more choice to accept or reject this change, we only need to adapt ourselves to the winds of change blowing across the digital world.

Ayush is the Founder of a Twitter community @SDGsForChildren that fosters the idea of digital citizenship for students by students. At the age of 14, Ayush founded this platform, where he helps children develop the necessary skills to find their voice and strive for a more just and equitable world. Schools and children across the globe are now part of this community with its own website, www.SDGsForChildren.org.

Ayush is an Indian Ambassador for the TeachSDGs project, initiated by the Global Goals Education Task Force, where he works in a group of over 100 distinguished global educators and shares his perspective and ideas on digital citizenship, social media, and technology use. He connects with global educators and contributes to meet Sustainable Development Goals. He is an active member of the TeachSDGs UN Communication Committee. He has also penned a book (under publication) that recounts his experiences, initiatives, and intense involvement in protection and promotion of human rights.

Ayush does not view digital media as a distraction from academics and other growth parameters. To him, the ever-evolving digital technology is an aid, rather than a barrier, to learning, in classrooms as well as homes. His initiatives involve setting specific goals, obtaining immediate feedback, and engaging Netizens constructively on digital media platforms across time zones.

Ayush is an inspiration that shows kids have a voice and they want to be heard. His passion for digital citizenship motivates students to reflect on their choices and how they can help the world even at a young age. His home has turned out to be a live example of how a family can use tech to be socially responsible citizens who can navigate the digital world to solve the problems of the real world.

A case in point is the story of Khushi, the seven-year-old daughter of a washerman in Ayush's residential society, who couldn't even calculate the number of clothes given to her for ironing as she was illiterate. When Ayush shared her plight with his mother, she encouraged him to teach her and eventually, they got her admitted to a school. Ayush also produced a YouTube documentary on Khushi entitled *Aaj Main Aasha Bo Aayi* (Planting the Seeds of Hope),[2] which created worldwide empathy for victims of lost childhood. This incident marked the beginning of Ayush's journey for "sowing seeds of hope" or the creation of equal opportunities for all inhabitants of the world.

Ayush's volunteering efforts received recognition when he represented

India at the 14th Youth for Human Rights International Summit held at United Nations headquarters, New York in August 2017. There he spoke on the urgency of putting an end to all forms of violation of human rights; killing of innocents, and injustice and exploitation of deprived humanity still rampant in many parts of the world. His speech received a standing ovation from the dignitaries and delegates drawn from across the world.

Ayush models proactive, socially appropriate, responsible ways that citizens can use to make the world a better place. He encourages fellow kids to use technology tools for a positive result, that is, to be good digital citizens. SDGsForChildren highlights the incredible capabilities technology can have on our society when it put towards helping and bettering the lives of others. This community includes schools and children from across the world who make innovative use of various digital tools such as social media platforms, blog, Skype, Flipgrid, Buncee, Skype, Padlet, and more to create a meaningful social impact by running various campaigns such as:

   •# *HumanRightsAndSDGs* – Under this campaign aimed at
   raising awareness about human rights in as many languages as
   possible, students are encouraged to design and share creative
   posters on any of the 17 UN SDGs.

   •# *SDGsGreenCampaign* – Children pledge to spread awareness
   about Earth Day under this campaign run for environmental
   protection. The activities undertaken under it include: online
   surveys on socially significant themes such as how children can
   contribute to saving the environment, and sharing their blog,
   picture or video, or anything which they think can make the
   Earth a more life-sustaining planet.

   •# *KeepTheHopeAlive* – The campaign underscores the point that
   children are never too young to act as catalysts of change in the
   world.

   •#*1MinuteWithSDGs* – Under this, students submit their one-minute YouTube video on any one of the 17 points of sustainable development.

• *# SDGsPosters* – An awareness campaign about human rights that asks students to submit posters on social issues such as fighting against bullying and racial discrimination.

• *# SDGsStories* – this campaign asks students to submit their short films on various social concerns.

Besides his mother, Ayush is also supported by his younger sister Ananya, a 10-year-old student of sixth standards, who acts as a responsible and responsive user of digital media in spreading the word about the need for ensuring basic human rights for all citizens.

Ananya displays rare ingenuity and innovativeness in taking to social media to highlight causes such as putting an end to discrimination, poverty, exploitation, injustice, and threats to the environment. She is also a Guest Blogger on www.wizardayush.com, along with her proactive and enterprising mother. "Our team champions the cause of digital access and connected learning opportunities for anyone anywhere including homes," explains Ayush with a proud smile.

Humanity needs more and kids like Ayush and Ananya gifted with innovation and leadership qualities to make this a better, more positive world for all of us.

The Chopra family, committed to modelling the SDGs, has shown that when you are passionate about creating change, you need to learn with the world and that going digital is the best medium to make it happen in a compassionate, kind way. The trio has opened up new ways to inspire students to embrace the digital citizenship or "global" society mindset in the true spirit of *Vasudhaiva Kutumbakam* (the world is one family).

Vasudhaiva Kutumbakam (the world is one family).

Connect with @jyoti1013, @Ayushchopra24, @WonderAnanya, and

@SDGsForChildren to continue to learn alongside this mother/son and daughter team.

CHAPTER FOUR
DIGITAL CITIZENSHIP IS GLOBAL CITIZENSHIP

MARY JALLAND, Scotland

Mrs. Jalland's Class Blog[1] and Teaching Global Citizenship Using Social Media and an Elephant[2]

Mary Jalland is a Primary Teacher in Scotland with a special interest in using social media to enhance learning and teach Global Citizenship. She is currently working on a Master's of Education in Early Years Pedagogue.

DIGITAL CITIZENSHIP IS GLOBAL CITIZENSHIP

Developing a sense of belonging in the world, a genuine identity of global citizenship and empathy towards those of differing cultures, can feel like no mean feat when you are teaching young children, some of whom have never and may never leave their own small country. The bottom line is that most children are not fortunate enough to travel the world, and those that do may never leave the confines of an airport or holiday complex. However, by embedding digital citizenship into my daily practice as a teacher, I have found that global citizenship falls neatly into place, whether it has priority in the curriculum or not. Quality learning about the world and our place in it can happen without ever leaving the classroom.

We have at our fingertips through our phones and computers ways to make us connected globally. But there is a troubling amount of ignorance and hatred towards those of different cultures evident through these platforms. I believe that teaching children to be responsible digital citizens will, in turn, make them good global citizens as they learn to communicate effectively and build relationships with people all over the world. To do this we need to start them young, so I would like to share with you how I explored this with my 4- and 5-year-old students.

IT ALL STARTED WITH A TOY ELEPHANT...

Whilst discussing aspirations with my class, it became increasingly evident that most of my students were unaware of the world outside their local community. I wanted to open their eyes to future careers that could make a difference to the world, understand what life is like for children globally, and develop respect and empathy. We have class mascots — three toy elephants named Ellie, Blue Ellie, and Granny Ellie who spend weekends with the children who tweet or write about their adventures. Reading Ellie's adventures is something that really engages the children, so we decided as a class to send Ellie further afield.

I had not anticipated the impact that this was to make, and we owe that to the person who kick-started our venture with such enthusiasm by taking our elephant to somewhere that was facing a major crisis. Dr. Janet Scott (a doctor who specialises in infectious diseases) took Blue Ellie to Sierra Leone and Liberia to fight Ebola.

You may think that teaching 4-year-olds about such an issue might scare them and that they are not old enough to comprehend such a devastating event, but I can tell you firsthand, the understanding and empathy that the children showed was astonishing. Dr. Scott tweeted photographs of the rigorous hygiene routines for the medical staff and the community, of the different kinds of professionals working together to fight Ebola, and Ebola survivors. In class, I shared these with the children who asked questions which we posted on Twitter, so there was an ongoing dialogue that extended their learning. The children learnt about the causes and nature of infectious diseases, linking their learning to their own experiences. They also learnt about the differing climates between different countries, and about food and the local community.

The quality learning didn't stop there. Through these tweets, our class started being followed by scientific researchers and medical staff from all over the world, so our questions were being answered and new ones posed. The children got feedback on their own science reports and experiments by real scientists, which inspired them further.

Suddenly the children who previously had few aspirations wanted to become medical professionals and scientists. The impact did not stop at the children in our class. Other classes and schools were also following closely, and parents were taking a keen interest in following the Ebola story on the news. On Dr. Scott and Blue Ellie's return to the UK, they visited our class, and that was a highlight of the school year. The connections made with scientists through this project led to learning about notable medical scientific researchers, and the children became #whywedoresearch ambassadors. The children were so inspired that it was the theme of their end of year assembly.

See our assembly trailer here.[3]

One of the wonderful things about social media is that by networking, more opportunities come about. The connections we made with the medical community led to the children asking how they could save lives, resulting in me teaching them how to do hands-only CPR. The role of digital media made this possible. I used YouTube to learn the skill myself. In turn, the children decided to make their own YouTube video to help them show others. Within a couple of days of posting this, we were getting messages from people all over Europe, and it was even shared in some medical conferences. This led to our school making professional videos with Save a Life for Scotland to be used in a training package. The children did not stop there. First, they taught everyone at the school. Then their parents came in to learn. Later they sent out a CPR challenge on Twitter, and now people all over the world have learnt to save lives using hands-only CPR as a result of this initial moment in the classroom. These children were certainly making a difference, and continue to do so.

See Ellie's CPR Challenge here.[4] Do join in.

Through this project, I hope you can see the value of social media in teaching the children global citizenship. Responsible digital citizenship was always modelled, so with continued work, hopefully sound digital etiquette will be ingrained by the time that these children are using social media unsupported. Social media is not just a place where people vent their ignorance, but a place filled with opportunities to learn about the world with the world, a place for kindness to be shared, a place that will inspire people to great social action.

Since the initial Ebola mission, our elephants have travelled the world, tweeting about the places they visit and about their work experience. They have been in the USA, Canada, Dubai, Germany, France, Afghanistan, India, and China to name but a few places. Our elephants have been historians, pilots, doctors, dentists, hairdressers, politicians, cleaners, council workers, and more.

Through connections made in West Africa, Blue Ellie got the call to join the British Army posted in Afghanistan. I admit I did think twice. Was this a mission too far to expose 4-year-old children to? After much thought and knowing that I had the control over which tweets to share with the children, I decided to go for it. After all, the children impressed me with their understanding of the Ebola crisis. The children again rose to the occasion.

In Afghanistan, Blue Ellie was photographed with soldiers and the Afghan police who were training to keep civilians safe from the shocking troubles going on. Through the tweets, we saw how a little boy was rescued from a Mosque that was under attack. The children also learnt about culture, religion, sport, climate, and wildlife in Afghanistan. This was all brought to life in our classroom through Twitter. Learning this way, rather than through direct instruction and textbooks, meant that the learning not only becomes more relevant, but it opens a world of intriguing facts to us. The National Sport of Goat Grabbing was an absolute gem of information that inspired the children to invent their own game of elephant grabbing. Who would have thought that such a difficult subject to teach would yield so much fun, and so much empathy and understanding? Again, it wasn't just the children learning, it was the adults too. Using social media to learn, helps us to learn together.

See our Sway on our learning on Afghanistan.[5]

Through these elephant adventures, and by linking via Skype and through social media, the world comes right to us in the classroom. So much is the impact that the children in one of my classes started referring to our interactive whiteboard as, "Our window into the world." That is an accurate description of how we use it. Through this window, the children have seen so much and connected with other children throughout the world. They have become aware of hardships facing millions of people less fortunate than they are. The Internet has revolutionised education, as we can investigate children's curiosities immediately. This year, off the back of an everyday conversation about how many toilet trips a day were necessary, we learned online the impact of no toilets and no clean running water in communities all over the world. This led to the children raising the money to build four toilets in communities in desperate need in Nepal, Malawi, Liberia, and Afghanistan. That's how the Internet can amplify student voice and why embedding digital citizenship enriches not only the children's education, but also our own education. Learning about the world with the world is the way forward.

Here is a Sway[6] compiling lots of our videos we have made on Global Citizenship. Enjoy!

It doesn't matter how old you are, where you live, what language you speak, we can all make a difference.

Connect with @ElliePrimary1 to continue to learn alongside this amazing classroom and classroom elephant.

CHAPTER FIVE
ALREADY IN PROGRESS

RACHEL MURAT, United States

All Things Social Studies[1] and Positively Social[2]

Rachel Murat has been an educator with the Maine Endwell CSD for 23 years. She is currently a social studies teacher and Tech Integrator at Maine Endwell High School in New York.

I've been blessed with a principal and superintendent that entertains my outside-the-box ideas and encourages me to push forward, so we don't become complacent. In 2013, I approached them about developing a Digital Citizenship course. We were just on the cusp of having carts and devices more readily available, and I really wanted to focus on how students could create, share, and show off their learning with the new devices we had. Six years later, that high school course has evolved into a Digital Leadership course where my students are not only examining their social brand, connecting online and offline actions, but creating and encouraging others to connect, create, and go beyond the four walls of their school, district, and community.

Now let's look at what we already have in progress in our classrooms, and spice it up a notch with some digital citizenship awareness!

Are you teaching an English Language Arts course? Why not have students write their free responses, creative writing responses, or free writes in a blog that can be shared beyond your four walls? Not only does this put their work out in front of others, but it also puts them in the creation mode instead of consumption mode. Blogging is not only something that is easily shared via social media or email, but it also makes it easier for your students to practice their feedback skills on each other's blogs. Giving both positive and constructive feedback is a skill that all students need to practice and why not give them ample opportunity! Don't look now, but you are modeling and practicing digital citizenship!

Are you teaching a social studies course? Why not crowdsource a Google My Maps where students not only demonstrate important mapping skills, but also learn to collaborate on a platform where it's important to make sure you honor the work of others? They could even do a class project where they have to plan out a "round the world trip," and one student's leg of the trip leads into another student's leg of the trip. They could connect with people in each of those countries and BOOM! The learning gets real! Not only are they practicing mapping and communication skills, but they are also practicing the skill of online collaboration. Don't look now, but you are modeling and practicing digital citizenship!

Are you teaching a global language course? Why not use social media to connect your class with one in a native speaking country where you share ideas, practice another language, and learn about one another's cultures? Once the students are connected, have them choose between a Flipgrid board where they communicate or write letters like our good-old, pen-pal days? Making global connections is so powerful for our students, especially those that are financially unable to vacation. Don't look now, but you are modeling and practicing digital citizenship!

Are you teaching a music course? Why not connect with some songwriters on social media or through Google Hangout (or Skype) and have your students collaborate to create a new piece of music? Not only are they practicing real-world skills, but they are also learning from a master musician! Never know when this will open up an internship opportunity for your students! Don't look now, but you are modeling and practicing digital citizenship!

Are you teaching a math class? Why not take the algebra (for example) that your students are learning and have them solve a real-world problem? Use your power on social media to look for a real-world problem where algebra (for example) can help out a group of people, village, etc. Don't look now, but you are modeling and practicing digital citizenship!

Are you teaching an earth science (for example) course? Why not have the students seek out a NASA scientist or hook up with the Space Station and have them take part in an experiment in real time? Don't look now, but you are modeling and practicing digital citizenship!

Is your Student Council celebrating International Day of Happiness? Why limit it to your campus? Spread the messages of the day by connecting with schools across the town, state, country, or globe. The connections and impact that the students make will last far beyond the one celebrated day of happiness. Don't look now, but you are modeling and practicing digital citizenship!

Are you holding an Open House or a Parent Night? Why not have students teach parents about positive uses of social media? You could show *Positively Social* (free on YouTube), have students teach parents how to use social media platforms, or just start a conversation about digital citizenship. Don't look now, but you are modeling and practicing digital citizenship!

Digital citizenship isn't one more thing. It's a work already in progress in your classroom.

In our Digital Leadership course, we've created tutorials, PSAs, blog posts, and resources that have been used by educators and students around the world. We've welcomed experts, coaches, college admission directors, teachers, authors, international speakers, and so many more from around the world into our class through Google Hangouts. We've hosted student-driven and student-led Twitter chats that celebrate kindness and show how students can, in fact, use social media for good. We've planned and hosted a Digital Citizenship Summit as well as planned and created the Positively Social video you will soon read about. We've helped raise funds and awareness for causes that we would have known nothing about if we had not been in a connected classroom focused on making an impact beyond our community. We've had guest judges from around the world for our presentations because we stream them through Facebook and Periscope. We've created portfolios that have earned scholarships, internships, and so much more for my students.

You don't have to have a class dedicated to digital citizenship and digital leadership to do all of these things, but why not take a risk and propose an elective course or put together an online course that is open source based? This way you can share your teacher/student created resources with the world! Once you connect with the world (or simply another school in your community), you won't look back!

I would be willing to bet that you are already in progress with many of these standards with the student creations in your classroom. Adding in the technology that will give the students the ability to go further than they had before, or even further than they thought possible, is where the magic happens. You are already doing great things, and character and citizen education are already part of what you are doing. Connecting those character and citizen conversations is a natural segue when you have technology in your classroom. Don't look now, but you are modeling and practicing digital citizenship!

> *Digital citizenship isn't one more thing. It's a work already in progress in your classroom.*

Connect with @MrsMurat to continue to learn alongside her.

CHAPTER SIX
STUDENT HELP DESKS

JENNIFER SCHEFFER, United States

Jenn Scheffer has been a business and computer technology educator for the past 18 years. She is passionate about digital citizenship education and providing students with real-world learning opportunities. She has presented on the topic of digital citizenship at state, regional, and national conferences and her work has been featured in several books on digital citizenship.

Burlington Public Schools in Burlington, Massachusetts has made digital citizenship education for all of its 3,400 students a district priority since its 1:1 iPad program launched in 2011. Rather than ban and block access to digital tools including social media, district leaders adopted the mindset that 21st-century students need digital citizenship education just as much as they need to learn the basics of reading, writing, math, and science. This education begins in the primary grades and lasts throughout high school. Upon graduating, with the help of innovative programming and risk-taking educators, students from Burlington are well-equipped to navigate an increasingly complex digital world in an ethical and savvy manner. They understand how to use a variety of digital tools to communicate digitally, the implications their digital reputation can have on their personal and professional lives, the importance of respecting intellectual property, why it is essential to abide by digital copyright laws, and how to use digital research strategies for their academic success.

Much of Burlington's success with digital citizenship education begins with the district's strong leadership. Burlington school leaders are savvy and active users of modern technologies themselves. They advocate for and support the use of progressive technology in the classroom. They know how to leverage tools such as Twitter, Instagram, and blogs to increase parent communication and promote the success of the district throughout the community. Through their own use of social media tools, Burlington leaders model for all school stakeholders what it means to be a responsible, contributing, and positive member of our digital world. They support curriculum which delivers real-world, authentic digital citizenship education. This results in a district culture where student voice is amplified, and collaboration becomes global. Burlington is a model district for other K-12 schools looking to develop or enhance their digital citizenship curriculum.

At the high school level, Burlington students have access to Instagram, Twitter, Facebook, and other 21st-century social media tools. They are reminded during a freshmen iPad orientation that what they post online is a direct reflection of their digital identity. All freshmen are required to take a self-paced, online course on digital citizenship featuring lessons on digital communication, information technology, digital safety and more. This introductory course lays the foundation for further, more sophisticated use of social media for their coursework. Students at the high school level also have the opportunity to enroll in a student Help Desk program where they are responsible for a globally-recognized blog and have the opportunity to participate in a live YouTube broadcast where they interview professionals in technology-related fields. The Help Desk course is formally titled *"Student Technology Integration and Innovation."* It is a semester-long course worth 2.5 credits and is available to sophomores, juniors, and seniors. The course description is as follows:

 The Student Technology Innovation and Integration course is a hands-on study of technology integration in an educational context. Students will be required to assess problem sets

throughout the day and define the best approach to addressing or solving the problem. In addition to solving problems for students and teachers, students will be required to complete and maintain several running projects that address problems or solutions in educational technology integration. The course also provides students with the opportunity to pursue an independent learning pathway in one of four areas: innovation, design, entrepreneurship or applications and develop a project which positively impacts their community. Students will be able to collaborate with outside businesses and organizations as they develop and implement their projects. To be successful in this course, students should have a prior understanding of Apple OS, Microsoft Windows OS, and the iPad iOS.

The Help Desk curriculum focuses on developing students' research, problem-solving, critical thinking, communication, and collaboration skills. Specifically, students are required to research, evaluate, and recommend the latest educational technology tools for teachers and students. Help Desk students have become reliable sources of information regarding the best technology to use for teaching and learning. In addition to app reviews, Help Desk students are well-versed in troubleshooting problems with software and hardware. Whether it is students needing assistance with updating their iOS, organizing their Google Drive files or Notability notebooks, or a teacher needing help with their projector or AirPlay, Help Desk students collaborate with one another to effectively and efficiently solve a wide variety of technical problems in the Burlington 1:1 environment. Another important part of the Help Desk curriculum is having students reflect on their learning through an individual blog. Students author weekly reflections on the skills they developed as a result of the hands-on nature of the course as well as the skill areas they want to improve upon.

The Help Desk program achieved national recognition for being entirely student-run and for leveraging social media tools to connect with other students and educators. Students involved in the program chronicled their learning experiences through their own individual blogs, and many of them were able to establish strong personal learning networks by using Twitter and LinkedIn.

A similar Help Desk program exists in Burlington at Marshall Simonds Middle School, and student-run Help Desk programs have developed all over the world; many of them look to Burlington as a model for curriculum and learning activities. Whether students are engaged in creating video tutorials explaining how to use various educational applications that are later published to the blog or presenting at educational conferences about the benefits of using social media to amplify student voice, a student Help Desk program is one way a school or district can create digital citizenship experiences for students that are relevant and meaningful.

At the elementary level, students in Burlington receive exposure to the concepts of digital citizenship primarily through using Google Classroom and Seesaw. These applications are closed, private, digital communities where the district's youngest learners gain knowledge and experience in digital communication and digital identity. They learn about the types of work that should be shared in a digital space, how to comment appropriately on each other's work, and how they can use digital tools to establish meaningful relationships with their peers and teachers. At the primary grades, lessons that emphasize digital safety are fundamental. Students must learn early on that they should never engage in a digital conversation with someone they don't know, should never share personal information such as their address or phone number, and should never give anyone their password. The advantage of digital citizenship education in the early grades is that students' mistakes can be corrected in a private space. Students can avoid certain behaviors that, if left uncorrected, could be detrimental to their future career or personal goals. Digital citizenship education at the elementary level is critical and requires a growth mindset on the part of educators. We owe it to our students to prepare them for an ever-changing, global society where digital technologies are used daily in most aspects of life. Failure to teach our early learners the concepts of digital citizenship is doing them a disservice whereas initiatives like DigCitKids are steps in the right direction. Students want to make contributions to our digital world, most of them are excited by technology, and with proper guidance and direction, they can channel that excitement in positive ways. I believe that given the opportunity to explore, create, and authentically use digital tools, students in today's classrooms can and will make a huge difference in the world of tomorrow.

> *Create a Help Desk program that meets the individual needs of your school community. Some programs focus on device repair and technical troubleshooting, while other programs focus on software or web tools. Your program might become a combination of the two or something entirely unique to your school district's needs. Gain the support from your school's administration before embarking on the development of a Help Desk program. Help your school administration see the value in having students take the lead with your technology initiative.*

Most importantly, connect your program to learning goals and sound curriculum. Keep your curriculum flexible and fluid. As technology tools change, so will the needs of your school community. For longevity purposes, build a program that can be easily adjusted to the rapidly changing world of technology. Finally, emphasize student voice regardless of the type of program you choose. Promote the work of your students on a blog or website. Help them develop their leadership and communication skills through blogging and/or social media and help them understand they are valuable school stakeholders and technology influencers.

For an overview of the BHS Help Desk program, see this video.[1]

Connect with Jennifer at @jlscheffer, @HelpDeskFH, and @The-BHSHelpDesk to continue to learn alongside her.

CHAPTER SEVEN
BUILDING CITIZENS IN MINECRAFT

MICHAEL DREZEK,[1] United States

Michael Drezek is the District Technology Integrator for Lake Shore Central School District in Angola, New York, serving as a teacher on special assignment. He has presented both regionally, nationally and internationally on topics related to educational technology.

We're all gamers. Think back to memories of your youth. My guess is many of those memories involve playing games with family and friends—from board games to sports to traditional family games and everything in between. Games bring people together. Games bring challenges.

Most importantly, games bring about fun. We learn so much through playing games including socialization, cooperation, strategy, learning how to deal with losing, learning how to win with grace, and sometimes learning how to deal with those who choose to play by their own rules. When I look at all of these, I can't help but make connections to the classroom and our education system. The rise of both gamification and game-based learning (GBL) illustrates that not only are educators hungry to find ways to engage learners, but also that they are tapping into something that many can relate to, and for all the right reasons.

Before writing this, I figured I would do a web search on popular games, in general, to see what came back. After a web search for "Popular Games," I scrolled and scrolled from one page to the next and could not find any results for non-digital games anywhere. The number one result returned led me to a list of 50+ video games[2] and the number one game on that list was Fortnite, a co-op sandbox survival game. The number three game on that list was Minecraft, a sandbox adventure game that originated in 2009 and currently has sold 144 million copies across all platforms and has 74 million active monthly users.[3] It was inevitable that something as popular as Minecraft over the last decade would eventually find its way to classrooms and ultimately to my lesson planning.

In the 2015-2016 school year, I was entering my 12th year as an educator and my second year as a technology integration specialist. Our Assistant Superintendent for Curriculum and Instruction, Melissa Bergler, shared about a local Minecraft Education workshop with our district. While she could have easily seen the word *Minecraft* and deleted the original email, she took a leap of faith in game-based learning and passed along the email to our entire school district, making the opportunity to attend open to all Lake Shore Central School District teachers. Math teachers Jacqueline Preischel and Nicole Wegrzynowski were the two who jumped at the chance. Again, it could have been another deleted email, but two teachers decided to take a risk for their students. Melissa, Jacqueline, Nicole, and I attended the full day MinecraftEDU workshop, and the rest was history. I will say that having the support of my Assistant Superintendent on this new adventure was key to bringing Minecraft to the classroom. She was right there learning along with us. Antonio Scordo, a Minecraft Education Trainer and a Regional Technology Coordinator for Erie 1 BOCES, led us through an initial pilot program. Initially, we used a Math World created by Antonio and his son. He aligned his Math World to our New York State Learning Standards. It included houses, gardens, pools, a conference center, a wizard's tower, and a free build area. Students learned about area, perimeter, and volume right within the game of Minecraft. It made the math stick because it made it visual. It was experiential. It was a beautiful thing.

The buzz in the room when students first spawned in the virtual world was priceless. As they solved math problems successfully, they earned building materials for the sandbox area of the world. Some chose to build solo while others teamed up with a friend. It didn't take long for a student to yell out, "Stop building in my space," and another to yell out that another student, "knocked down some of their builds and took some of their building materials." Griefing! That was the word I had never heard before Antonio shared it with us in the initial workshop. Now I was living it. Despite establishing some ground rules, simply telling students to be respectful to one another in the game was not enough. Consider this a teacher fail. However, this experience also helped me have a bit of an a-ha moment. If students could establish the rules for their own classroom with success at the start of a school year, why couldn't they be empowered to establish their own rules for their virtual space in Minecraft just the same? One of my favorite features (and likely the students least favorite) of MinecraftEDU is the ability to "freeze" all students in-game simultaneously. Doing this allowed us to regroup and start an important conversation. It helped students to realize that they needed to participate in the virtual world just as they would in the real world. They established the following expectations:

- Respect all players' builds
- Only take what you need
- Keep the world clean
- Keep chat messages positive and necessary
- Keep calm and craft on

These student-led, student-generated expectations set the table for a successful experience. It wasn't perfect, and at times students needed to be reminded by their peers of the guidelines they created, but it was important that a few slip-ups served as teachable moments.

Once we saw the excitement over Minecraft Edu from our students, we had to do more with it. I was lucky to stumble on a Tweet from Marco Vigelini, a teacher and CoderDojo leader from Italy, in April of 2016.

As part of this global art project in Minecraft Edu, schools from around the world take physical artwork and import it into a virtual replica Louvre museum. Our students shared their drawings, paintings, sculptures, and more. Many of these items were representative of their culture and community. Students also were given a plot of land to build out a virtual community with things that represented their school and local community. This activity made such an impact on me that the students' creations are captured from the Minecraft sky in my Twitter profile banner to this day. They built a US flag, a pixel art eagle to represent our Lake Shore mascot, a rainbow beacon to represent inclusiveness, a bounce house to represent having fun, and a Seneca Nation wampum belt to represent our Native American community. They also built the community in snowy conditions to represent our Western New York winters. It amazed me to watch our students be incredible digital citizens when exploring other schools' virtual art and builds. At any time they could have broken a block, shattered glass of the replica Louvre, or built-in another school's community. None of this happened. There was a high level of mutual respect and appreciation among the participating schools. At one point, our classes were able to connect on the server at the same time. This put their digital citizenship to the test. Students were able to say hello over messaging in Minecraft. They complimented each other on their artwork. They would have stayed online all night had it not been time to catch the after-school bus home. I am confident these students won't forget the experience. The world certainly felt smaller when schools from Japan,

Italy, Australia, Canada, Israel, and the US were able to learn from each other through art and creativity in the same Minecraft world.

Read more about the project here.[4]

Our Minecraft Edu journey would not stop here. It also led us to a Skype Classroom lesson from Minecraft inspired author and student, Sean Fay Wolfe. Sean authored books in the series *The Elementia Chronicles*.[5] He shared his journey and how his passion for gaming led him to write. Our students realized that they too could write stories based on their Minecraft creations. Our students asked great questions, including one that dealt with players who "troll" others and cause grief within the game. Sean shared his own experiences and explained how some of his books' characters were built around people he has encountered online. It didn't take long for our school librarian to stock the shelves with Sean's books. They are a huge hit, and the personal connection makes reading them that much more special for our students.

Our school is now using Microsoft Minecraft Education Edition. I have found nothing but support from the community of Global Minecraft Mentors. Currently, teachers can find a community of over 500 lesson plans created by educators around the world on the official website. Lessons include Language Arts, Science, Math, History & Culture, Art & Design, and Computer Science. This year our students will take part in a Minecraft Education Sustainability Shuffle, focusing on the United Nations Sustainable Development Goals. The project is led by Canadian educator Benjamin Kelly. Regardless of the activity, lesson or project, Minecraft Edu and other online games provide the perfect opportunity for students to craft their digital citizenship skills. It sets the stage for important conversations to be had, a safe environment for mistakes to be made, and lessons to be learned.

Professional gaming is now a reality. League of Legends World Championship Semifinals matches sold out Madison Square Garden's 18,000+ seat arena on back-to-back days in 2016. While the odds of turning this hobby into a career might be stacked against most, one can't ignore the fact that Varsity e-sports teams are popping up in high schools. Robert Morris University was the first college to offer scholarships for gaming, offering up to $19,000 per year.[6] It is likely that most students will not go down this path. However, students can benefit from being exposed to the benefits of Minecraft Education in the classroom. I'm a supporter of the exploration, creativity, discovery, collaboration, and curiosity that Minecraft incites in learners. These are skills that can be experienced in a digital space yet applied in any walk of life.

Game-based learning has crafted a new perspective on teaching and learning for me, and I am grateful for Minecraft Education for opening my eyes to this. I am also grateful for having a space that allows students the opportunity to craft their digital citizenship and ultimately their citizenship as a whole. They won't always get it right, but they will be given the opportunities to get it right because of educators who are willing to take a risk and try something in the classroom that others might run away from. Please continue to share any digital citizenship experiences through gaming with the hashtag #bethatKINDofgamer and #bethatKINDofkid.

Connect with @m_drez to continue to learn alongside him.

To get started[7] with your own Minecraft Edu, check with your technology department on access to Minecraft: Education Edition, which requires Microsoft Office 365 accounts. Teachers can install Minecraft Pocket Edition on tablets if they don't have Windows 10 or Mac computers.

CHAPTER EIGHT
ARE YOU CONSUMING OR CREATING?

CLAUDIO ZAVALA, United States

I Am Claudius[1]

Claudio is an edtech coordinator and consultant based in the Dallas-Fort Worth area who passionate about fostering creativity in the classroom and using creation tools to enrich learning and experiences in the classroom. He's an Adobe Education Leader, Alpha Squirrels, Flipgrid Ambassador, Google Certified Educator and a Participate Community Advisor.

We figuratively and **literally** have access to information at our fingertips! For example, when I needed to fix our 2001 Honda Civic brake light switch, we searched online for a step-by-step video on how to replace it. So cool! I'm sure I'm not the only one who's searched for images for clarification, instruction, or general interest.

With it being so easy to look for images or videos, I think it is becoming equally easy to use photos or graphics as our own on social media, classwork, or personal branding. However, because it is easy to search and find an image online, it doesn't mean we have a right to use that image. Much less make revenue off that photo!

CONSUMING

> **con·sum·ing**
> /kən'soomiNG/ ◂))
>
> adjective
>
> (of a feeling) completely filling one's mind and attention; absorbing.
>   "a consuming passion"

2

We are all consumers! We purchase items for nutrition, fuel for our vehicles and school supplies for our students to use! There's nothing wrong with being a consumer. We all need to eat. In addition to consuming natural supplies, we have become Digital Consumers. We watch Netflix, YouTube, and other Social Media content. As Digital Citizens, we can easily feed ourselves on a steady diet of watching, watching, watching, and never realize we are not contributing!

As Digital Citizens, we want to teach our students best practices that will help them properly curate and create content. Consuming can easily put us in a predicament of violating copyright laws. For example, students will search for images via Google or Bing, and add it to their report without giving credit to the owner. Another scenario has a student copying an image from the web and adding text, and then sharing on a social media platform—never realizing they are infringing on the photographer's rights!

There are resources to help you teach students about copyright and fair-use laws. You can find these lessons on Common Sense Media's[3] website.

Here are several ideas and tools you can use to help your DigCitKids be content creators, rather than consumers.

CREATING

> **cre·ate**
> /krē'āt/ ◂))
>
> verb
> gerund or present participle: creating
>
> bring (something) into existence.
>   "he created a thirty-acre lake"
>   synonyms: produce, generate, bring into being, make, fabricate, fashion, build, construct; More

4

I'm a big proponent of creating and using your own content. As a creator, both students and you have control over how to use images, graphics, or videos. Also, if students ever want to monetize their creations, they can do so!

To help DigCitKids shift from consumers to creators, show them ways they can create content. There are many digital tools or apps they can use to do this. Depending on your students' age, they can use their own devices or school devices. Let's explore two Adobe apps they can use to create graphics and videos.

ADOBE SPARK POST

Adobe has engineered a tool that makes sharing your own story easy! I believe an important part of being a DigCitKid is being able to not only tell others what you are about, but share them!

Post takes design tools found in advanced applications and simplifies them, giving students the power to design and create beautiful and eye-catching graphics. Spark Post helps students create global collaboration theme content rather than consume. In it, they can use their own or shared photography (selfies, landscapes, or portraits) within their graphics. This helps them tell stories, to positively impact their school, community, and world. Students can collaborate on a piece to amplify their voice. Here's an example of a student acrostic poem.

ADOBE SPARK VIDEO

A sibling of Spark Post, Video offers DigCitKids the option to tell their story using motion imaging instead of using static graphics. Students can create high-quality videos.

Film and video are powerful mediums to share one's story! It offers an engaging way to communicate and message a story. Instead of searching YouTube, Vimeo, or other video services, DigCitKids can collaborate and script a short story via Google Doc and then create a movie using Spark Video. In minutes, they can combine their own video clips, photos, and icons provided within the tool into an engaging video story.

ADOBE SPARK PAGE

The third offering in the suite of Adobe Spark apps is Page. Spark Page provides students a place to write their stories to share among classmates and friends across the world.

DigCit Kids can create journals and compose stories as ways to share their experiences. Page's interface easily lets students add content such as images, graphics, and videos they create. Students can then publish their Page to the web via a shared link for others to view. Students across continents can share their Pages.

The Adobe Spark apps offer DigCitKids a way to become creators of images and videos. They become the designers and editors of their own print or digital media. Students are the photographers, directors, editors, and producers of their own content. Now others will watch and listen to their stories, changing the students' perspective from Consumer to Creator! Need some ideas and lessons using Adobe Spark? You can find exemplars and lessons for Adobe Spark Post and Video at https://edex.adobe.com/spark.[5]

Help students learn to create rather than just consume. Be the photographer, director, editor, and producer of your own content.

Connect with @ClaudioZavalaJr to continue to learn alongside him.

CHAPTER NINE
WHO WILL YOU SAY YES TO?

Amy Storer,[1] United States

Amy Storer is an instructional coach and lead technology integration mentor in Montgomery, TX. She loves being an instructional coach and working alongside the wonderful educators of Keenan Elementary School. She is a distinguished educator that encourages and motivates others to reach far beyond the classroom walls to make learning more meaningful and inspiring. She has a true passion for working with other educators and students to empower them to make and foster global connections.

#Make200. This is where it all started for me as a connected educator. I had just created my first classroom Twitter account, and when we hit our 200th follower, we decided to thank her on Twitter. Little did I know that this moment would cause a ripple of impact for my students and me.

"I just finished my AM swim. Can you draw a pool with [a] perimeter of 200? What's an appropriate unit?" When I read this aloud to my fourth-grade students, they were in disbelief that someone whom they had never met was asking them to help with a math problem. I can remember hearing one of my students say, "Do you think she will say anything back?" They were so motivated to answer this question just to see if Dr. Julie Jones would answer. Thinking back on this, I often wonder if they would have been as motivated if I would have asked them the same question. Would they have dropped everything they were working on to focus on this? Maybe. Here is what I think made the difference for them. She was our authentic audience. This made a huge difference for my kids. It was such a meaningful experience for them, and they craved more of it. They wanted to make those connections, and who was I to stand in their way?

Julie was the match that lit the fire for us. Soon after meeting her, we formed a close relationship, and my fourth-grade students worked with her undergraduate students a couple of times to show them all about augmented reality and classroom management. Even though we were in Texas and the college students were in South Carolina, her college students were an integral part of our classroom. Because of her, I was motivated to reach out to others to support my students and their interests. For so long, I thought that it would be impossible to get an expert to visit with my kids, but the worst they could say was no, right?! That was my thought when I reached out to local meteorologists in the Houston area. I wanted to connect my kids with them so they could explore weather maps further. I never heard back from anyone. This deflated me. I decided to go on YouTube to find a video about weather maps, and I came across a video by Ryan Davidson. He had created it for his niece and her class to learn more about weather maps. I decided to take a risk for my students, and I searched for him on Twitter. In less than 48 hours, he responded! I was able to connect him with my students, and the experience was unforgettable. At the time, I had no idea who he worked for, but found out pretty soon that he worked for The Weather Channel! We just needed someone to say yes, and he was that someone for us. He even visited with my class the next school year when he was working for Weather Underground. I will be forever thankful that he said yes.

As a Project-Based Learning (PBL) facilitator, I knew the importance of connecting my students with an authentic audience. One of the first PBL experiences that we worked on was inspired by Kevin Honeycutt and Ginger Lewman. If it weren't for Twitter, I would not have met either Kevin or Ginger, since they are located in Colorado and Kansas. We were approaching a unit in fourth grade on rocks and soil, and I reached out to the two of them for some guidance on how to create a meaningful PBL experience for my kids. It didn't take long for Kevin Honeycutt to respond with not one, but two graphics for my students to choose from. Once again, we were many miles away from each other, but he was someone that said yes to my students. Thank you for saying yes. Because of the two of them, my students were able to "take a trip to Mars" and get connected with a Martian soil expert. The entire experience was meaningful and engaging for my students.

Even after leaving the classroom to become an instructional coach for my district, it's still the connections that continue to impact and change me as an educator. Being a connected educator is more than just having a social media account. It is about surrounding yourself with people that grow you and lift you up. It isn't just about tearing down your walls to connect with other states, it's also about tearing down your own walls to connect with those in your building. We all have so much to share and such great things to highlight. I appreciate these individuals and so many more who just said yes to me and my kids. Who will you say yes to?

> *Becoming a connected educator was one of the best decisions that I've ever made. The first step that I took was to create a Twitter account and then follow educators that had already made an impact on me. That one small step has taken me so far. Take that step and create a Twitter account to connect to classrooms and educators from all over the world. And don't forget to get connected in your school, city, and state!*

Connect with @techamys to continue to learn alongside her.

CHAPTER TEN
THE POWER OF
PORTFOLIOS

MANDY FROEHLICH, United States

Leadership, Innovation & Divergent Thinking[1]

Mandy Froehlich is the Director of Innovation and Technology for a school district in Wisconsin where she supports and encourages educators to create innovative change in their classrooms. Her passion lies in reinvigorating and re-engaging teachers back into their profession, as well as what is needed to support teachers in their pursuit of innovative and divergent thinking.

We have high aspirations for our students. We know that any one of them at any point could be the person who cures cancer or invents time travel. But, we send them off to a non-structured life at college when three months prior they had to ask to go to the bathroom and weren't allowed to access social media at school, let alone taught how to create real change using their voices. If we want students to change the world, we need to give them resources, knowledge, and skills to be able to write and speak in that space.

When I was in the classroom and my colleagues were teaching their students to create paper portfolios, I had the idea that each of my students would create their portfolios on their own Google Site. We had just gone 1:1 with iPads and I was trying my best to learn how to integrate them with intention. I searched YouTube and figured out how to make a site template, shared it with my students, and asked them to set goals and reflect on pieces of their work according to their core subjects, how they functioned within our classroom community, and a personal goal. The students did everything I asked. Still, at the end of the year, I looked back at the portfolios and knew they weren't exactly what I had envisioned, yet I wasn't sure how to change the format of the digital portfolios. The issue was that I was missing two important pieces: experience and purpose.

While every teacher's focus should be student learning, I have always believed that teachers need to continue to learn and grow as well to create meaningful learning experiences for their students. One of the best ways to enrich student learning is to focus on teacher professional learning, reflections, and passions. So, while this book focuses on digcit kids, my chapter is focusing on the teacher perspective to enhance the student experience. In my experience, they're so closely linked that it would be difficult to separate them out.

FROM THE TEACHER'S PERSPECTIVE

Outside of the large binder of artifacts and reflective pieces that I had put together for my pre-service college teaching program, I had never kept a true professional portfolio let alone a digital one. I had no experience in what I was asking the students to do. It wasn't until I moved out of the classroom that I started my own digital portfolio, so it is only through hindsight that I was able to see where I missed the mark. True reflection, the kind that should go into a portfolio, needs to be explicitly taught and takes repetitive practice. Frequently, we ask students to be reflective, but we don't actually teach them how to do that — how it sounds in our heads while we are reflecting and how it feels when we are organizing our thoughts and pushing our thinking. It is not an activity to be done three times a year, which was what I had my own students doing. The ability to be truly and deeply reflective is developed over time, and we can only teach our students to do this fully when we are participating in the activities ourselves.

Many times people make assumptions about my relationship with writing because of my blog (my reflective piece of my professional portfolio). They use these assumptions as reasons for why I can write but they can't. These usually are:

Writing comes naturally to me.

It does not. I did not excel at writing in school, I never wrote poetry as a child, and it's not even really an interest of mine. I write to get my ideas out and to organize my thoughts. I don't need to be passionate about it to understand it serves a higher purpose.

Full of epiphanic ideas

I'm not. I have honed the skills of listening to conversations, being aware of what's happening around me, and noticing my thinking to come up with ideas for reflection. I keep lists when a topic comes to me. This is another skill I've practiced.

Not busy

I am just as busy as everyone else. Because I have come to realize that this reflection helps me both personally and professionally, I make it a priority, and we always make time for the things that are important to us.

What I've realized that while I reflect, I am organizing my thoughts in a way that makes sense in order to write them down. When I write them down, I am creating what I like to call "brainspace" because I am getting the unorganized thoughts that are rolling around out of my head. This brainspace allows me to spend more time on ideas or issues that are happening both personally and professionally, and takes some of the stress out of overthinking situations. But again, I have had to practice this repeatedly to make it work for me in this way.

Finally, I needed to build up the courage to share my thinking with the world by making my portfolio public. Usually, I hear teachers say something like, "Why would anyone want to hear my ideas?" but if you're asking that question, it's the wrong one. When it comes to our professional thoughts, the question should be, "How can I give back to my professional learning community on a larger scale after all they've done for me?" There will always be someone who finds your ideas to be creative and new no matter how redundant or uninspired they seem to you. If we say we want to be a part of a worldwide learning community, we need to take our responsibility to give back to that community seriously. One way to do that is to keep a public professional portfolio where your PLN can follow your thinking and ideas.

BACK TO STUDENTS

When working with students now, I have come full circle having experience and purpose. I've practiced what I'm asking for students and have found purpose in why I would ask them to keep a digital portfolio in the first place. I understand that while some students may naturally be more reflective than some, reflection is a skill that is not inherent and needs to be taught and practiced.

Also, keeping a digital portfolio with regular reflection will allow them to look back and see the difference in both their thinking and their writing. I often go back to my original posts and cringe, but the difference between my first post and my latest post is *growth*. Teaching students to see how their thinking and writing changes over time is not only a skill, but also shows them that recognizing growth is as important (if not more important) as a grade. Especially for students who may never get an "A" or achieve a four, seeing growth gives them something to celebrate and be proud of.

If we want students to change the world, we need them to contribute their thoughts in that space. Otherwise, the perception is that their work and ideas can't make a difference to anyone but the teacher and for anything but a grade. Many times when students contribute on a larger scale, it's thought of as an extra, that it was awesome that students were involved in their community. Actually, this should be the expectation because our students are expecting to make a difference. They are watching others be the catalyst for change all the time on YouTube and online. We need to be the ones to provide them the vehicle to begin developing and organizing their thoughts as the foundation for moving forward with action.

PRACTICAL TIPS FOR BEGINNING

Getting started on a heavily front-loaded project is always the biggest challenge, but those also seem to have a high return on investment as well and in the end are worth the work. Here are some tips for beginning and maintaining both professional and student portfolios:

Choose your platform carefully.

In the ideal educational world, when it comes to digital portfolios, there would be one (free) site that houses classrooms of portfolios from grades K-12. It would have a switch at about 4th and 8th grades that would allow for a more robust user interface. At twelfth grade that switch would allow the student to take all their years of hard work and take it with them to be used for college entrance or to continue their reflection beyond high school. It would also have a professional portfolio component attached that would be geared towards teachers. I have yet to find this program, even though I've discussed this issue with multiple edu portfolio companies.

Professionally, I use WordPress which is easy and fast for creating and publishing, but gives me enough options to expand on my portfolio. Edublogs works on the WordPress platform and gives the teacher the ability to set up and see all the student blogs from a dashboard. Edublogs with access to all of its pro features is not free at the district level. It can be used simply for free with limitations. Another issue with Edublogs is that the user interface is too difficult for little ones to use quickly. If the initial shell of the portfolio is set up for the students, I think Edublogs could be used in grade four, possibly grade three. For high school students, a benefit of Edublogs is that the portfolio can be easily exported into CampusPress (their college/university version) or WordPress for the students to take with them after graduation.

There are many other portfolio sites to choose from. Bulb is another site that allows for classroom management, similar to Edublogs, but is not free. Many of the teachers in my district have used a combination between Seesaw for the lower grades and then Google Sites. While this isn't ideal, it is free, and the Google Site can be used by the student as long as they are in school. Another option made by Google would be Blogger. The benefit of Blogger would be that the teacher could be put on as an author each year and therefore have the ability to quickly have access to each portfolio (a little bit of a daunting task for secondary, but still a workaround).

When choosing a platform, keep in mind that technology is changing every day. While it's important to put thought into which platform you'd like to use, the platform isn't as important as what you will create with it and the learning that happens as you go. It's not the tool, but how you use it that matters.

Implementation

The first step is learning how to choose the platform you use. Familiarity with how the site works reduces anxiety about whether a post goes out at the intended time and if it is formatted correctly. In my experience, this is often where the portfolio-specific learning stops. However, two important pieces of learning still need to happen. First, students need to be taught to deal with the fear and anxiety that naturally comes along with sharing their thoughts and ideas publicly. Discussing these ideas openly and voicing their internal dialogue will help. I also often recommend the video *Obvious to You, Amazing to Others* by Derek Sivers,[2] not only for students but for teachers too. It describes our natural feelings of believing our ideas aren't good enough to share and how others might find our ideas amazing, and is a great segue into the discussion.

Next, the art of reflection needs to be taught and practiced. Begin with reflecting on simple things like an assignment and move to deeper reflection about bigger ideas. Model reflection as to how it allows us to organize our thoughts and come to conclusions about our thinking. How do themes in our thinking show our biases? Beliefs? Assumptions?

Allow times for students to reflect on what they want to reflect on. This will allow them for more buy-in to the process. If all they reflect on are assignments given by the teacher, they may come to resent it.

Finally, write down thoughts as you go through the process of starting your own professional portfolio, so you don't forget what it's like to start. Sometimes, as we become more adept at something, we forget the challenges of beginning. In this case, it may be more difficult to remember how terrifying it can be to press "publish" on that very first post. As teachers, we don't want to forget what that feels like so we can empathize with the students and give them the strategies we used to move forward. Keeping notes or a video diary on this process will help us do that. Maybe start a Flipgrid[3] with the process that either you or students can refer to later.

Maintenance

From a professional standpoint, as you become busier, it is going to be a challenge to keep going. There will be times where you just don't feel like writing and where it doesn't seem to be a priority. Here are a few tips for working through those times and to keep moving forward:

1. Choose a realistic posting goal: I began with once a month, then went to once every three weeks as I became better and quicker at writing. I posted more if I could. Now, I post once a week. Choose something that works for you. If you begin with a goal of twice a week and continuously fail, you may be more likely to quit the process altogether.

2. Put it on your calendar: I add writing time into my calendar to be sure I have the time to do it, and I remember.

3. Write when you can: If you have a few ideas and have some time, write multiple posts. Keep them in draft form. Even if they are just outlines of posts, they will be easier to fill in later. That way if there is a week where you don't have time, you still have a post to publish.

4. Writing on the go: I spend a large amount of time in my car. I will often either use speech-to-text in a Google Doc or leave myself voice messages on Voxer. Then, when I'm ready to publish a post, I will either go back to that Google doc, clean it up, and post it or I will dictate the Voxer message I left. Either way, it allows me to utilize my time more efficiently in case I'm not in front of my computer at the moment I have an idea for reflection.

5. Pay attention: Every conversation, experience, and memory is an opportunity for a reflective piece. Keep a list with short descriptions in a Google Doc or Keep to reference later.

With both student and professional portfolios, consistency is key. Posting regularly will grow your readership as people begin to know when the posts will be out and expect them.

Many times when we think of digital portfolios, we focus on the artifacts - proof of learning. However, the artifacts are not the end goal; they should simply be one of the topics of reflection. The reflective piece of the digital portfolio is what will ultimately allow both professionals and students to see our thinking, look for biases and assumptions, and create goals and look for growth. If we are asking our students to change the world, we need to be the ones to show them how it's done, and digital portfolios are one of the vehicles to give them a platform to begin.

If we want students to change the world, we need them to contribute their thoughts in that space.

Connect with @froehlichm to continue to learn alongside her.

CHAPTER ELEVEN
STUDENT VOICES IN A GLOBAL CLASSROOM

JoAnn Jacobs, Hawaii

JoAnn Jacobs teaches sixth-grade social studies at Mid Pacific in Honolulu, Hawaii. She and her students have been learning about the world through the UN's Sustainable Development Goals for the past four years.

A quilt is made of up of many different pieces of fabrics that are various textures, colors, and design. This is the best way I can describe what my classroom has been like over the past five years teaching sixth-grade social studies. Each year has been different; each class has its own distinct personality, interests, and voice.

When I think back over this special time in my life, my thoughts always return to the strength of my students' voices. They decided what we would study and how they would present their learning both in the classroom and to an authentic audience, continually practicing the tenants of good digital citizenship. Living in the middle of the Pacific Ocean made connections outside of our classroom a critical point of student learning.

A partnership that truly benefited my students was made through the Peace Corps. We exchanged videos and emails with a small high school in Indonesia in helping the students practice their English. In a time when ISIS was in the news daily, our partnership brought about a different understanding of what it meant to be Muslim.

Another connection made was through my friend, Julie Hembree, a librarian in Seattle, Washington. We were matched with a fourth-grade class in Lesotho, a small country located within South Africa. Again we exchanged photos and videos, and when our books were returned to us due to the teacher's inability to pay an exorbitant tax, a group of sixth-grade girls volunteered to read and record books which were placed on our YouTube channel for all students to view.

The largest and most popular project over the past few years has been the UN 2030 Global Goals. Research is a critical part of student work, and therefore once again good digital citizenship is the key. Students, after selecting their own topics, need to be sure their information is both reliable and current. One of the questions that continually surfaced was "how can the problem be solved?" We continually discussed and decided bringing awareness would be a good first step. So over the next few weeks, we used the design thinking process to develop products which would bring focus to each issue.

In between the design thinking process and sales so many other things happened.: constructing prototypes, accepting criticism, deciding on a final product, defending the choice during a Shark Tank-style presenta- tion, earning fifteen dollars to purchase supplies while at Walmart, keeping a balance sheet, investigating an agency to receive profits, and construction and preparing for the final sale.

The sale took place during the middle school lunch period with groups divided up over five days so individual groups would have one day to explain their cause and sell what they made to students and teachers.

This is just a snapshot of what life is like in my sixth-grade global classroom. Each day is different. Some are better than others, but the continual focus is being good digital citizens connecting with the world.

Many times those beginners give up because they take on more than what they can possibly accomplish. In order to build global partnerships, look for one that will fulfill the expectations you have for student learning and stick with it. Get to know the person you will be working with and continually communicate so you can readily develop ideas together and reach the goals and objectives you have for yourself and your students. Once you have the initial experience, you will be able to grow your network and both join and build quality projects.

Connect with @JoAnnJacobs68 to continue to learn alongside her.

CHAPTER TWELVE
BUILDING BRIDGES,
CONNECTING CLASSROOMS

OLUWAKEMI OLURINOLA, Nigeria

Oluwakemi Olurinola is an educational technologist, Microsoft Innovative Educator Fellow, Skype Master Teacher, TeachSDGs ambassador, and Digital Citizenship Institute Associate who teaches about the world with the world through a variety of tools that help her connect students in Nigeria around the world with other classrooms.

The world, without doubt, has become more interconnected, and coming from a developing country, it has become imperative that we educate our students to become globally competent, to develop the skills and know-how needed to live, learn, and work in this global village.

One of the major milestones on my journey as a global educator and digital citizen was when I got introduced to and joined the then Microsoft Partners in Learning Network, which is now the Microsoft Educator Community. Being a part of such a global community of educators broadened my horizons and exposed me to global best practices. I began connecting with educators from across the globe, building a diverse and dynamic professional learning network. These led to collaboration and more connections across other social media, following and building followers. Another milestone for me was getting introduced to Skype in the Classroom, which gave me the opportunity to engage with classroom and students across the globe, visiting places that would have been practically impossible but for Microsoft Skype in the classroom platform. Through Skype, my students and I embarked on learning about the world with the world, which earned me the recognition as a Skype Master Teacher. Living in a country challenged by inadequate technology infrastructure in schools and a lack of affordable Internet connectivity, armed with just a laptop and a hotspot, I have been able to break down the classroom walls and connect students to classrooms across the globe. The delight on the faces of these students when they come ether realization during the connection that they are more alike than different from the kids in other parts of the world gives me the ultimate satisfaction I get from making these connections happen at all odds.

Connecting dots, I came in contact with the Digital Citizenship Institute at a Microsoft Experience Centre during ISTE. Where I was introduced to Marialice by my Skype Program Manager, it so happened that she found out Marialice would be in my country in a few weeks from then and thought we just had to meet. That meeting has further broadened my global connectivity. Being a digital citizen removes land borders, emphasizing commonalities and challenging students and all to use technology for good.

As we make these global connections, our students need to be aware of what it means to be digital citizens and how to successfully navigate and interact within the digital space. Making such connections and learning about diverse people and cultures help them come to understand that our value systems are similar—values such as respect for one another, and showing kindness and empathy, among others, are global needs. And they also learn to appreciate differences where they exist. As educators, we need to raise students who are globally-minded because the present technology advancement is blurring our countries borders and global skills are in demand.

SKYPE IN THE CLASSROOM

Skype in the Classroom helps foster connected learning in a connected classroom. It is an online community that enables thousands of teachers to inspire the next generation of global citizens through transformative learning over Skype.

SKYPE LESSON

Skype Lessons are a specific lesson about a particular subject given by an expert on the subject matter. It is normally given in a presentation format with the speaker talking into the camera and also possibly using screen share and taking Q&As.

MYSTERY SKYPE

Mystery Skype is an educational game that connects two classrooms who are somewhere in the world. Teachers will know where (and who) they're calling but students will not. The goal of Mystery Skype is to locate the other class geographically. Students must ask Yes/No formatted questions.

INVITING A GUEST SPEAKER

Teachers can request sessions with Guest Speakers if they think their background and experiences will work for the subjects they are teaching.

VIRTUAL FIELD TRIP

Virtual Field Trips are when experts 'out in the field' take students on an experience that is specific to their location, e.g. tour guides, explorers, marine biologists, zoologists and scientists

SKYPE COLLABORATION

Skype Collaborations are projects or Skype Lessons created by teachers to connect their classroom with another classroom around the world. Skype Collaborations can make learning global EVERYDAY for students and empower them to act in ways that are meaningful to them. www.skypeintheclassroom.com

---

So break down those classroom walls, make that connection, collaborate, invite a Skype guest, take a virtual trip, play mystery Skype with a class on another continent, and learn about the world with the world.

I believe that every child, regardless of parental income or background can and should benefit from the gains of technology-enhanced learning. We need to provide life-transforming opportunities for our students, preparing them for the challenges of the 21st century, providing in every possible way equal chances to succeed both in school and beyond.

I look forward to building networks with people across sectors and of different countries, to develop global competence and intercultural learning, and to look into the possibilities of connecting and collaborating, synergizing to align the global competence need across sectors and countries.

> *Being a digital citizen removes land borders, emphasizing commonalities and challenging students and all to use technology for good.*

Connect with @kolurinola to continue to learn alongside her.

CHAPTER THIRTEEN
AUTHENTIC LEARNING

Tracy Mercier,[1] United States

Tracy is a Library Media Specialist at a Connecticut Magnet School, and she is also a Responsive Classroom Consultant. Her goal to develop empathetic communicators extends beyond the Library Media Center as the Chief Content Creator for the Digital Citizenship Institute. You can follow Tracy on Twitter, Instagram and YouTube @vr2ltch where she shares more of her ideas for working with children.

As educators, we are tasked with educating the two largest generations ever—Generations Z and Alpha. Both generations have grown up with technology, although slightly differently, creating the largest generation gap since Baby Boomers hit the scene. While Gen Z (last graduating class is 2028) continues to quickly adapt to the ever-evolving tech, Gen Alpha was born with an iPad (both arrived in 2010). For most of us, this just means we *expect* to communicate with each other—via text, video calls, or social media. For our students, technology is more than that; it is not a tool but a singularity in their lives.

Our students are constantly connected, and the global access that technology provides has not only made them the smartest generation ever, but also the most empathetic. Global access allows them to rapidly expand their knowledge, meaningfully connect with others, be more aware of global issues, generate and seek solutions (at younger and younger ages), and impact global change. They will be the most transformative generation ever. They will leverage the world.

This requires us to radically rethink education. We are on the right path, and yet have much work to do to effectively engage our students. While many schools have increased technology purchases and are integrating the use of technology into curriculum, an alarming 35% still need to provide Wi-Fi access (Costanza, 2015).[2] Our students want more than access to technology. They need more than being able to play educational games on a device. They expect more than writing a paper in Google Drive.

How do we as educators support our students' global impact efforts?

- Create 1:1 environments through purchases and/or BYOD
- Ensure a strong Wi-Fi connection that can handle a multiple user load
- Design relevant and meaningful learning opportunities that use technology in a way that redesigns learning
- Allow students to hack school—design their own projects, learning experiences, classes, and majors[3]
- Provide student choice
- Personalize learning
- Increase digital resources

What does this look like in action? Invite students to use technology to solve the problems of drought or food shortages. They can become investigative journalists who uncover FastFashion issues and propose both cost-effective and civil alternatives. Our youngest students can share digital documentation of the best part of themselves as a way to celebrate diversity and self-worth. Have them share their voice about social injustices (locally and/or globally) on Twitter chats. Most importantly, listen to their interests and pay attention to how they are using technology.

One of the great things about social media is the ability to connect with others around the world. Using social media in the classroom invites students to solve real-world problems in real time. What a great way to demonstrate empathy while utilizing critical thinking skills!

GETTING STARTED

• Choose a platform that's right for the age you teach and the times you teach in and available technology. Empatico, GoBubble, and Seesaw are great platforms for under 13s. Empatico connects classrooms around the globe to share similarities and differences with everyday life experiences and the impact those experiences have on us. GoBubble connects students in a way that mirrors Snapchat, Twitter, and Instagram. Seesaw is a great portfolio platform for students to share their learning and learn how to comment on each other's work.

• Connect face-to-face expectations and rules to the online world. It can be tempting to create new rules for how we behave online, and it is important that our students know that how we treat people and conduct ourselves is what's important. If a rule is to treat others with kindness, then that rule should be taught, followed, and endorsed in the classroom and online.

Keep learning authentic. It can be tempting to create lessons that focus solely on digital citizenship, but these skills can and should be embedded into everything we do every single day.

Connect with @vr2ltch to continue to learn alongside her.

CHAPTER FOURTEEN
DIGCIT ANYWHERE

EUGENIA TAMEZ, México

Eduktech[1]

Eugenia Tamez is the founder of Eduktech and is the mother of three teenage girls. She is passionate about educational technology and digital citizenship. As a consultant, she is leading México towards a new perspective regarding the positive use of educational technology and digital citizenship in schools, companies and public institutions.

DigCit anywhere, anytime...being a digital citizen is our natural form of living.

I first heard about digital citizenship about six years ago accidentally while I was looking for some educational apps for my girls' school. As a mom of three teenagers, technology use with tablets, smartphones, and games was starting to become part of our everyday life. While I was researching how to educate my kids on technology use, I found a new MOOC about a completely different topic, *Digital Citizenship*, created by Dr. Jason Ohler.[2] It looked interesting, so I signed up. At the same time, the school was starting to use technology with seventh graders. The school's principal asked me for advice on apps to develop creativity and engagement,. That's when I had a moment of inspiration

— I started Eduktech, a research and consulting company that would offer, among other services, digital citizenship education services.

As I conducted research about how to engage and educate students about using technology, I realized that something else was missing. Students needed something else, not just the best apps, programs, or educational tools to help them learn content. They needed to know how to use technology creatively, responsibly, and wisely. They needed to know how to be digital citizens.

I spoke to the school principal, who had almost no interest in adding digital citizenship to the curriculum or talking about it with students and teachers. In his eyes, I had created a dilemma for which the school didn't want to take responsibility.

From whom do kids need to learn about digital citizenship? Some may say that it's a part of today's parenting; others may say it's the responsibility of a foundational K-12 education. The reality is that digital citizenship is so vast that parents, educators, and community leaders need to play a role.

Digital citizenship is our new way of living because technology use is part of everyday life. No matter if our children are in school, at home, with friends or by themselves, they need to know how to be safe in cyberspaces. They need to know how to respect others' property and interact responsibly online. They also need to know how to make a difference using the Internet and the tools of the Digital Age to benefit humankind.

We need to guide and train new generations on important issues like:

- Understanding that technology allows us to make important connections; if it's not used wisely, it may disconnect us from our beloved ones and our real-life connections.

- Understanding that using technology is a matter of time management; we need to be able to determine which tech activities deserve our time. Not all screen time is equally valuable.

- Understanding the rights and responsibilities of tech use.

- Understanding how to build the digital footprints we want our children to have to represent themselves on the world stage.

The Internet, artificial intelligence (AI), virtual reality (VR), and social media haven't been used educationally until recently. Our students are now leading the use of new technologies, challenging our schools to catch up with them. We need to hear them and make them part of our efforts to use digital technologies to shape the world that we all want. Everything is changing, so it is urgent for us to keep up and restore humanity to the use of such technologies. It might sound scary or even menacing, but it doesn't have to. We can change our mindset and see it as a big opportunity. Let's not be afraid. It is our job to educate and guide new generations on how to navigate in the digital era.

Above all, we need to start now to make our technology human, and not make the mistake of taking out humanity out of technology.

In México in particular, I definitely hope that as technology use is increasing, so will the interest in digital citizenship. New generations are interested in positive technology use, but we need to provide this information and educate them on a massive scale. I know it's not easy in a country where many basic needs are still not satisfied, but technology can help communities. With the positive use of technology, younger generations can stand out and make their contributions for a better México.

Humanizing digital generations is something we need to do every day. It doesn't matter where you live, or what language you speak because digital citizenship is about human connections online.

CHAPTER FIFTEEN
ONE WORLD, ONE CLASSROOM

Bronwyn Joyce, Australia

Our Global Classroom[1]

Bronwyn is a teacher from Traralgon, Australia who specialises in Curriculum Innovation and the delivery of training, linked to critical and creative thinking and bringing the world into classrooms. She is an advocate for the United Nations Sustainable Goals and believes we live in a world where we should be learning together. Her Our Global Classroom mission statement is simple – One World, One Classroom.

 We live in a world where education depicts the future of its successors.

As educators, teaching allows us to change the lives of children, to make them worthy citizens; show them how to be empathetic and to prepare them for the future.

There is a big world just waiting to be explored. If educators don't innovate the curriculum and integrate the world into their classrooms, some children will never, ever know there is actually a world out there that they can be part of.

- Our Global Classroom

This quote catapulted my passion for globalising my own classroom and classrooms around the world. Bringing the world into a classroom allows our students to build student agency, amplifies student voice, and develops students who are Future Ready.

My journey began the moment technology took my classroom to places I never imagined or expected. My students were Skyping world artists like Joel Bernger,[2] using his artwork to connect them to refugee camps. They were also reading books linked to asylum seekers and following the journeys of refugees all around the world. Students were also participating and leading global projects through iEARN[3] and other global platforms.

As teachers, we need to empower our students to lead their own learning. For me, this was a big step, and I started simply by using rich digital media to create "Look to Learn"[4] tasks that helped develop critical thinking habits with my students. Every week the students would be given a task linked to a global image with open-ended questions. In class, we worked in literacy sessions on commenting on a blog. This is an important teaching moment linked to digital citizenship. Students need to be explicitly taught how to comment on a blog; otherwise, we give them a license to respond inappropriate ways.

The 'Look to Learns' were as simple as the example below. Taking a global video or image, adding critical thinking questions. My students were engaging with real-world issues in our classroom without even knowing. I was following the curriculum doing these tasks in reading and writing sessions. My students' levels of engagement accelerated due to their curiosity about what was happening in the world.

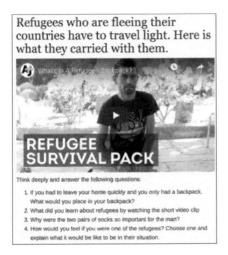

Refugees who are fleeing their countries have to travel light. Here is what they carried with them.

REFUGEE SURVIVAL PACK

Think deeply and answer the following questions:

1. If you had to leave your home quickly and you only had a backpack. What would you place in your backpack?
2. What did you learn about refugees by watching the short video clip
3. Why were the two pairs of socks so important for the man?
4. How would you feel if you were one of the refugees? Choose one and explain what it would be like to be in their situation.

Invite the world into your classroom by starting a blog. Begin by posting 'Look to Learn' tasks for your students.

In 2015, the United Nations launched a new campaign to bring awareness to issues surrounding the world and sustaining its development. The United Nations identified 17 Global Goals,[5] with a target to reach these achievements by 2030. I didn't know about the Global Goals until 2017 when I found them while updating the curriculum with global resources. My students were already tackling big issues facing our world through our 'Look to Learn' work, so it was easy to integrate the Global Goals and have students develop a call to action.

I connected with Mareike Hachemer[6] who was passionate about the Sustainable Goals and had prepared resources that would support classrooms to begin their journey. Her work just made integration simple. I needed to start with getting the students to prepare their own 17 goals. If they were going to understand the goals the United Nations wanted them to achieve, they needed to understand the issues the world is facing. I decided to do some reverse psychology in my classroom. I asked the class to:

List the most severe problems happening in the world today.
THEN
Create 17 goals to solve these problems you have identified.

Using the following model developed by Mareike Hachemer, the students came up with goals I had not even considered, such as things like safe homes, protecting kids, friendship, and no fighting. The world was facing all these problems, but the kids I teach were experiencing their own issues every day. I realized I needed to work harder and I needed to recognise these goals fitted perfectly with the sustainable goals.

Working with the DigCitInstitute and international colleagues globally, I designed tasks, met with experts, and promoted the work my class was working on through social media. I challenged district protocols in countries, had students campaigning in their schools, and I had people talking about these goals. It was happening, but who was leading this? My students, NOT me, but the kids I was teaching.

Our Global Classroom, which is what my class calls itself, saw students writing information reports about the goals, making videos using Flipgrid to amplify their voices to people around the world on global goal topics, and tweeting out posters and messages to world leaders to make them listen. These kids were change-makers, and they were leading their own learning to get others to follow their lead. The students in Our Global Classroom were inventing, innovating, and campaigning, mirroring the United Nations Sustainable Goals.

In 2018, Our Global Classroom (OGC) broke down barriers around the world. The OGC Flipgrid[7] houses more than 50 tasks linked to the United Nations Sustainable Goals. Thanks to co-pilots Michael Drezek and Malinda Hurts over 200,000 people have interacted with the grid, and teachers all over the world use the tasks to spark critical thinking in their classrooms.

We need to unite, share our passion. There are too many lone soldiers working in schools around the world taking risks with learning, allowing students a voice, and creating change. I say to you all, keep doing what you are doing. Push the boundaries, give kids the opportunity to explore the world, and bring the world to them because too many of our students may never see the world for themselves.

Our work will never be done; every day something new happens that will inspire new thinking. Aim for students to be Future Ready by taking learning beyond the classroom walls: supporting the implementation of the United Nations Sustainable Global Goals in classrooms and students leading their own global collaboration projects.

As we reflect back to my own words, I began the chapter with –

 We live in a world where education depicts the future of its successors.

As educators, teaching allows us to change the lives of children, to make them worthy citizens; show them how to be empathetic and to prepare them for the future."

Join us on the OGC Flipgrid (previously mentioned) and share your voice with the world as we collectively solve the world's most daunting problems together.

CHAPTER SIXTEEN
FINAL THOUGHTS

Now, let's think about the future. With emerging technologies — augmented reality, virtual reality, mixed reality, machine learning, artificial intelligence — our world is changing at such a rapid pace that we need to ask if we are preparing our children and students for their future?[1]

Will our students be ready? It's up to us to ensure they are DigCit Ready.

This is why, in today's interconnected world, digital citizenship is everyone's responsibility.

Our big takeaway after reading all of these contributions is that we need to be willing to learn alongside each other. All we need to do is provide the opportunities and invite others into this critical conversation at home, at school, and at work. The easiest way to start is to learn *with* students, colleagues, family members, and other community members.

We need to rethink how we learn, unlearn, teach, and parent, and how we can embed empathetic, entrepreneurial, inclusive, and innovative mindsets into our everyday lives. We hope you'll take the tips from each chapter and begin to explore ways you can embed these skills, dispositions, and mindsets into your regular routines. Take the DigCit-

Kids message and pass it on by *experiencing* digital citizenship together and inviting others to join you.

We are in this together. It doesn't matter what language you speak, where you live, or what religion you practice — digital citizenship is all about community and an opportunity to inspire and empower others to take action and become changemakers in their own communities, because once you make an impact locally in your own backyard, it has a ripple effect and continues to influence global and digital communities.

How will you make a DigCitImpact at home, at school, at work?

OTHER EDUMATCH BOOKS

EduMatch Snapshot in Education (2016)
In this collaborative project, twenty educators located throughout the United States share educational strategies that have worked well for them, both with students and in their professional practice.

The #EduMatch Teacher's Recipe Guide
Editors: Tammy Neil & Sarah Thomas
Hey there, awesome educator! We know how busy you are. Trust us, we get it. Dive in as fourteen international educators share their recipes for success, both literally and metaphorically! In this book, we come together to support one another not only in the classroom, but also in the kitchen.

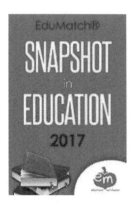

EduMatch Snapshot in Education (2017)
We're back! EduMatch proudly presents Snapshot in Education (2017). In this two-volume collection, 32 educators and one student share their tips for the classroom and professional practice. Topics include culture, standards, PBL, instructional models, perseverance, equity, PLN, and more.

Journey to The "Y" in You by Dene Gainey
This book started as a series of separate writing pieces that were eventually woven together to form a fabric called The Y in You. The question is, "What's the 'why' in you?" Why do you? Why would you? Why should you? Through the pages in this book, you will gain the confidence to be you, and understand the very power in what being you can produce.

The Teacher's Journey by Brian Costello
Follow the Teacher's Journey with Brian as he weaves together the
stories of seven incredible educators. Each step encourages educators
at any level to reflect, grow, and connect. The Teacher's Journey will
ignite your mind and heart through its practical ideas and vulnerable
storytelling.

The Fire Within
Compiled and edited by Mandy Froehlich
Adversity itself is not what defines us. It is how we react to that adversity and the choices we make that creates who we are and how we will
persevere. The Fire Within: Lessons from defeat that have ignited a
passion for learning is a compilation of stories from amazing educators
who have faced personal adversity head on and have become stronger
people for it. They use their new-found strength to support the
students and teachers they work with.

EduMagic by Sam Fecich

This book challenges the thought that "teaching" begins only after certification and college graduation. Instead, it describes how students in teacher preparation programs have value to offer their future colleagues, even as they are learning to be teachers! This book provides positive examples, helpful tools, and plenty of encouragement for preservice teachers to learn, to dream, and to do.

Makers in Schools

Editors: Susan Brown & Barbara Liedahl

The maker mindset sets the stage for the Fourth Industrial Revolution, empowering educators to guide their students to pursue a path of learning that is meaningful to them. Addressing a shifting culture in today's classrooms, we look to scaling up and infusing this vision in a classroom, in a school, and even in a district.

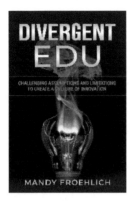

Divergent EDU by Mandy Froehlich
The concept of being innovative can be made to sound so simple. We think of a new idea. We take a risk and implement the new idea. We fail, learn, and move forward. But what if the development of the innovative thinking isn't the only roadblock?

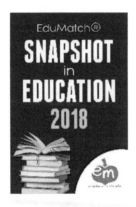

EduMatch Snapshot in Education (2018)
EduMatch® is back for our third annual Snapshot in Education. Dive in as 21 educators share a snapshot of what they learned, what they did, and how they grew in 2018. Topics include purpose, instructional strategies, equity, cultural competence, education technology, and much more!

Daddy's Favorites by Elissa Joy
Illustrated by Dionne Victoria
Five-year-old Jill wants to be the center of everyone's world. But, her most favorite person in the world, without fail, is her Daddy. She wants so much to share her ideas, her creations, and most of all, her time. But Daddy has to be Daddy, and most times that means he has to be there when everyone needs him, especially when her brother Danny needs him. Danny is exceptional. He is talented. He is special, and he steals the attention she wants the most. And although Daddy doesn't mean to, sometimes he asks her to share Jilly-Daddy time.

Level Up Leadership by Brian Kulak
From Mario to Lara Croft, gaming has captivated its players for generations and cemented itself as a fundamental part of our culture. Regardless of the genre or platform, one immutable fact connects gaming heroes and the gamers who assume their identities: in order to reach the end of the game, they all need to level up.

NOTES

PREFACE

1. *DigCitImpact*: when digital citizenship is embedded into everything we do by changing mindsets through an empathic, entrepreneurial, inclusive and innovative mindset.
2. Africa's Next CEO. www.facebook.com/AfricasNextCEO/

1. DIGCITKIDS: OUR STORY

1. "Digital Citizenship Institute." http://digcitinstitute.com/. Accessed 15 Dec. 2018.
2. "DigCitKids." http://www.digcitkids.com/. Accessed 15 Dec. 2018.
3. Voxer. "Walkie Talkie App for High Performance Teams." Walkie Talkie App for Team Communication I Voxer, www.voxer.com/.
4. https://sites.google.com/a/gonevr2l.com/theexplorerssite/&sa=D&ust=1546449780477000&usg=AFQjCNHECvjSGN6Vklct-Os3dhmwiwkBm_Q
5. "The Utter Joy of Curiosity - Marialice B.F.X. Curran - WordPress.com." https://mbfxc.wordpress.com/2011/04/03/the-utter-joy-of-curiosity/. Accessed 2 Jan. 2019.
6. Curran, Marialice BFX, and Regina G. Chatel. "Virtual mentors: Embracing social media in teacher preparation programs." Pedagogical applications and social effects of mobile technology integration. IGI Global, 2013. 258-276.
7. https://sites.google.com/a/gonevr2l.com/theexplorerssite/home/lostering-with-our-friend-jerry-pallotta
8. "Geocaching." https://www.geocaching.com/. Accessed 11 Jan. 2019.
9. "Jules Verne - Wikipedia." https://en.wikipedia.org/wiki/Jules_Verne. Accessed 2 Jan. 2019.
10. "The Tweet Seen Around the World I - Marialice B.F.X. Curran." https://mbfxc.wordpress.com/2013/11/01/the-tweet-seen-around-the-world/. Accessed 15 Dec. 2018.
11. "Around the World with Curran: Where in the world are you?." 3 Nov. 2013, http://aroundtheworldwithcurran.blogspot.com/2013/11/where-in-world-are-you.html. Accessed 15 Dec. 2018.
12. "How to Write a Quality Comment! - YouTube." 9 Oct. 2010, https://www.youtube.com/watch?v=UDVSw54VU1A. Accessed 2 Jan. 2019.
13. "Comments4Kids." 20 Feb. 2016, http://comments4kids.blogspot.com/. Accessed 2 Jan. 2019.
14. "Connected from the Start – Primary Preoccupation - Kathy Cassidy." http://kathycassidy.com/connected-from-the-start/. Accessed 2 Jan. 2019.
15. "Around the World with Curran: Animals in the Rainforest." 28 May. 2014, http://aroundtheworldwithcurran.blogspot.com/2014/05/animals-in-rainforest.html. Accessed 2 Jan. 2019.
16. "Total Trust - Marialice B.F.X. Curran - WordPress.com." https://mbfxc.wordpress.com/2011/08/27/total-trust/. Accessed 2 Jan. 2019.

17. "DIGCITSUMMIT | DigCit Institute." http://digcitinstitute.com/digcitsummit/. Accessed 2 Jan. 2019.
18. "Timmy Sullivan #GreenNewDeal (@TimmySull1van) | Twitter." https://twitter.com/timmysull1van. Accessed 2 Jan. 2019.
19. "Tyler Clementi's Story • Tyler Clementi Foundation." https://tylerclementi.org/tylers-story/. Accessed 14 Jan. 2019.
20. "Dinosaurs and Tiaras: Facing Intolerance | - Marialice B.F.X. Curran." 27 Apr. 2011, https://mbfxc.wordpress.com/2011/04/27/dinosaurs-or-tiaras-facing-intolerance/. Accessed 14 Jan. 2019.
21. "High School Skype and Twitter Project Request |." 13 May. 2011, https://mbfxc.-wordpress.com/2011/05/13/high-school-skype-and-twitter-project-request/. Accessed 15 Dec. 2018.
22. "#iCit21 - YouTube." 9 Feb. 2012, https://www.youtube.com/watch?v=vgmZLXQL-NPQ. Accessed 15 Dec. 2018.
23. "CT-N: iCitizenship Town Hall Meeting on Bullying at St. Joseph College." https://ct-n.com/ctnplayer.asp?odID=7450. Accessed 11 Jan. 2019.
24. "The Global Read Aloud." https://theglobalreadaloud.com/. Accessed 2 Jan. 2019.
25. "Marialice B.F.X. Curran, Ph.D. on Twitter: "Absolutely! When ...."" 13 Nov. 2018, http://twitter.com/mbfxc/status/1062367544504475649. Accessed 15 Dec. 2018.
26. "Lessons Learned Going Device Free #digcit | - Marialice B.F.X. Curran." https://mbfxc.wordpress.com/2016/06/06/lessons-learned-going-device-free-digcit/. Accessed 14 Jan. 2019.
27. https://www.youtube.com/watch?v=dJjR8GWXXKA
28. "Digital Government Strategy | US Department of Transportation." 3 Aug. 2018, https://www.transportation.gov/digitalstrategy. Accessed 15 Dec. 2018.
29. "December is DigCitKids Approved #digcit4kidsbykids #bethatKINDofkid." 2 Dec. 2017, https://medium.com/@digcitkids/december-is-digcitkids-approved-digcit4kidsbykids-bethatkindofkid-ab99e57f534a. Accessed 2 Jan. 2019.
30. "Learning Together: DigCitKids & Cyber Seniors | #DigCitUtah." https://digcitutah.com/digcitkids-cyber-seniors-learning-together/. Accessed 2 Jan. 2019.
31. https://www.youtube.com/watch?v=-S-5EfwpFOk
32. https://www.youtube.com/watch?time_continue=1&v=HF-a-UmoRt4
33. https://docs.google.com/presentation/d/1xHWwn0Cp_Ab22WF8E1B0KJep7Lk-Y0Ns4yEsDyQPTLVI/edit#slide=id.g46819e7cc5_0_93
34. https://docs.google.com/presentation/d/1DIX2qd-RbZPk1_XnngswNLLy-BLZ4Jxy44lNmQAsEWHo/edit#slide=id.g255aee7188_0_6
35. "Petition · Mayor Sylvester Turner and City Council of Houston: Bag ...." https://www.change.org/p/mayor-sylvester-turner-and-city-council-of-houston-bag-free-bayous-houston. Accessed 15 Dec. 2018.

2. BEING A CONNECTED PARENT

1. https://www.iwomanish.com/
2. "According to the FBI, Knives Kill Far More People ... - The Daily Caller." 19 Feb. 2018, https://dailycaller.com/2018/02/19/knives-gun-control-fbi-statistics/. Accessed 15 Dec. 2018.

3. THE GREAT INDIAN DIGITAL FAMILY

1. "SDG teaching tools & child-friendly materials I The 2030 Agenda for ...." https://www.unicef.org/agenda2030/69525_82235.html. Accessed 15 Dec. 2018.
2. https://www.youtube.com/watch?v=fy5We4La11c

4. DIGITAL CITIZENSHIP IS GLOBAL CITIZENSHIP

1. https://blogs.glowscotland.org.uk/fa/mrsjalland/
2. https://sway.office.com/Rh3QGqWio3PHfZzJ?ref=Twitter
3. https://youtu.be/1ek0JGO4HRM
4. https://sway.com/DMWzk2WfF96pieMe
5. https://sway.com/CVsezVUAxZzyL71J
6. https://sway.com/Rh3QGqWio3PHfZzJ?ref=Link

5. ALREADY IN PROGRESS

1. http://spartansocialstudies.blogspot.com/
2. https://www.youtube.com/watch?v=BTMIryyR-nI&t=2s

6. STUDENT HELP DESKS

1. https://www.youtube.com/watch?reload=9&v=L5fwFTuAjek&feature=youtu.be

7. BUILDING CITIZENS IN MINECRAFT

1. https://michaeldrezek.com/
2. "The 50+ Most Popular Video Games Right Now." *Ranker*, 2018, www.ranker.com/list/most-popular-video-games-today/ranker-games.
3. Aernout. "Minecraft Sales Reach 144 Million Across All Platforms; 74 Million Monthly Players." *Wccftech*, Wccftech, 22 Jan. 2018, wccftech.com/minecraft-sales-144-million/.
4. https://stateoftheart.creatubbles.com/2016/09/22/a-journey-into-creativity-with-creatubbles-and-minecraft/
5. "The Elementia Chronicles #1: Quest for Justice: An Unofficial Minecraft ...." My Book. Accessed 15 Dec. 2018.
6. Scholarships.com. "Esports Scholarships / Scholarships for Gamers." *Scholarships for College Free College Scholarship Search 2018-2019*, www.scholarships.com/financial-aid/college-scholarships/sports-scholarships/esports-scholarships-scholarships-for-gamers/.
7. "Get Started I Minecraft: Education Edition." https://education.minecraft.net/get-started/. Accessed 20 Jan. 2019.

8. ARE YOU CONSUMING OR CREATING?

1. https://iamclaudius.com/
2. https://www.google.com/search?safe=active&surl=1&q=consuming+definition&
rlz=1C1CHBF_enUS754US754&oq=consuming+definition&aqs=chrome..69i57j0l5.
3095j1j7&sourceid=chrome&ie=UTF-8
3. "K–12 Digital Citizenship Curriculum Scope ... - CommonSense.org." https://www.
commonsense.org/education/scope-and-sequence. Accessed 15 Dec. 2018.
4. https://www.google.com/search?surl=1&safe=strict&rlz=
1C1CHBF_enUS754US754&ei=yE8aXMjUF8eyggfwwqrIAQ&q=create+definition&
oq=create+definition&gs_l=psy-ab.3..0j0i7i10i30j0i7i30j0j0i7i30l6.151602.153440..
153590...2.0..0.99.614.8......0....1..gws-wiz.......0i71j0i67.aVpcLffbuE8
5. https://edex.adobe.com/spark

9. WHO WILL YOU SAY YES TO?

1. https://linktr.ee/techamys

10. THE POWER OF PORTFOLIOS

1. https://mandyfroehlich.com/
2. https://www.youtube.com/watch?v=xcmI5SSQLmE&feature=youtu.be
3. "Flipgrid." https://flipgrid.com/. Accessed 14 Jan. 2019.

13. AUTHENTIC LEARNING

1. "vr2ltch." 21 Dec. 2018, http://www.vr2ltch.com/. Accessed 14 Jan. 2019.
2. "Educator Innovator | What Does It Mean to Be "Future Ready ...." 7 Apr. 2015,
https://educatorinnovator.org/what-does-it-mean-to-be-future-ready-adaptable-
for-starters/. Accessed 14 Jan. 2019.
3. "Pigzbe: Helps Kids 6+ Develop Great Money Habits by ... - Kickstarter." https://
www.kickstarter.com/projects/primotoys/pigzbe. Accessed 14 Jan. 2019.

14. DIGCIT ANYWHERE

1. https://eduktech.net/
2. "Jason Ohler Free MOOC on Digital Citizenship » D & D Tech." 10 Jan. 2014,
https://ddtech.sd62.bc.ca/2014/01/10/jason-ohler-free-mooc-on-digital-
citizenship/. Accessed 2 Jan. 2019.

15. ONE WORLD, ONE CLASSROOM

1. "Our Global Classroom – One World One Classroom." https://
ourglobalclassroom.com/. Accessed 15 Jan. 2019.
2. "Joel Artista | Joel Artista: nomadic artist, educator & advocate for social ...."
https://joelartista.com/. Accessed 15 Jan. 2019.

3. "iEARN-USA." http://www.us.iearn.org/. Accessed 15 Jan. 2019.

4. "Look to Learn – Our Global Classroom." 19 Nov. 2018, https://ourglobalclassroom. blog/category/look-to-learn/. Accessed 15 Jan. 2019.

5. "The Global Goals." 9 Sep. 2018, https://www.globalgoals.org/. Accessed 15 Jan. 2019.

6. TEDx Talks. "Empowering Educators for the Global Goals! | Mareike Hachemer | TEDxHeidelberg." YouTube, YouTube, 4 Jan. 2017, www.youtube.com/watch?v=u5OcbNTqbM4&feature=youtu.be.

7. "Flipgrid - Video for student engagement and formative assessment." https://flipgrid.com/whatif. Accessed 15 Jan. 2019.

16. FINAL THOUGHTS

1. https://www.youtube.com/watch?v=HF-a-UmoRt4